Enameling *with* Professionals

Enameling
with
Professionals

by Lilyan Bachrach

EDITORIAL TEAM
Elizabeth Bachrach Tan, PhD
Barbara Bachrach Scolnick, MS
Martin Communications
Benjamin I. Bachrach, PhD
Robert Z. Bachrach, PhD
Laura Ruth Scolnick, PhD

BOOK DESIGN - Julie Murkette
JACKET DESIGN - Barbara A. Buttler
PRINTING COORDINATOR - Gary A. Gurwitz, Mercantile/Image Press, Inc., West Boylston, MA
COLOR REPRODUCTION - Rebecca Lange
ENAMEL TECHNICAL ADVISER - Woodrow Carpenter, Thompson Enamel, Inc.

© 2002 by Lilyan Bachrach. All rights reserved.

Published by Lilyan Bachrach, 4 Rossalare Drive, Worcester, Massachusetts 01602 USA

First Edition

ISBN 0-9719252-0-8

No part of this book may be reproduced in any form or by any means without prior permission of the Copyright owner except in the case of brief passages embodied in critical articles and reviews written for publication or broadcast.

Lilyan Bachrach, the contributor writers, and anyone connected with the publication of *Enameling with Professionals* disclaim any responsibility or liability for damages or injuries as a result of any use, activity undertaken or application of information contained in this book. We are not responsible for the use of materials or equipment mentioned in this book. It should be understood there is always a need for precautions and knowledge required to use any material or equipment.

Printed in the United States.

Acknowledgements

When I was half way through the book my younger daughter reminded me that she had once told me that writing was hard work and time consuming. Fortunately, I had not remembered. I am blessed to have literate, knowledgeable family members who were willing to help me edit this book. Without them, my editorial team, I would never have been able to complete the task.

Tim McCreight detailed for me what was involved in publishing a book. I was fortunate to find what I call my staff of wonderful people to work with who encouraged me in this effort. They filled the positions that he outlined I would need and their names and fields are listed. To all of them and the enamelists who have been so helpful, I say "thank you."

*To my husband of fifty years, Samuel Bachrach, M.D.,
I dedicate this book.*

*He was always my best critic, encourager and booster.
He loved the well-written printed word and a quality bound book.
I think he would have been proud of this one.*

Preface

You are now holding *Enameling with Professionals*, a delightful, informative and very important addition to enameling literature. You will not only be excited and rewarded seeing the work of so many eminent, contemporary artists who work with enamel, but you will be forever grateful for their "how-I-work" procedures to execute one of their favorite techniques.

Lilyan Bachrach, a veteran enamelist of almost fifty years, has been tireless in collecting and editing the material for *Enameling with Professionals*. Each artist has responded graciously and unselfishly resulting in this book that you will read and refer to many times. Future artists working with enamel will enjoy the benefits of this book just as much as the present enameling community and the admirers of enameling artistry.

Woodrow Carpenter
Chairman of the Board, Thompson Enamel

Table of Contents

Introduction 15
The Enamelist's Vocabulary 19
Enameling Workshop 21
Karat Gold Alloys 27
  Stuart Grice
Metals For Enameling 33
The Manufacture of Enamels 39
  Woodrow Carpenter
The Enamel Material 41
Techniques for Beginners 51
Paisley Design 54
  Doris Hall

Enameling Techniques

Overglaze Direct Painting 59
  Lilyan Bachrach
Plique-à-Jour: Russian Soldering Method 65
  Sandelle/Sandra E. Bradshaw
Cloisonné Beads of Fine Silver 69
  Linda Crawford/Linda Crawford Designs
Enameling on Sterling Silver 75
  P. Alexa Foley, M.A.
Gold Alloys: Champlevé and Bàsse-Taille 79
  Edward J. Friedman
Gold Cloisonné Wire on Fine Silver 83
  Falcher Fusager of Magick/Fusager-Demski Design
Stencils and Watercolors 85
  Jenny Gore

Illustrations

Overglaze Direct Painting - *Bachrach* 89
Plique-à-Jour: Russian Soldering Method - *Bradshaw* 90
Cloisonné Beads of Fine Silver - *Crawford* 91
Enameling on Sterling Silver - *Foley* 92
Gold Alloy Enameling - *Friedman* 93
Gold Cloisonné Wire on Fine Silver - *Fusager* 94
Stencils and Watercolors - *Gore* 95
Paisley Design - *Hall* 96
Foils: Fine Silver and 24K Gold - *Hunter* 97
Decals and Ceramic Pencils - *Jasen* 98
Large Mosaic Enamels - *Jenkins* 99
Enamel Crayons - *Killmaster* 100
Champlevé with Ferric Chloride - *Komrad* 101
Portrait with Enamel Watercolors - *Kuller* 102
Torch Firing - *Lozier* 103
Vessel Forms - *Perkins* 104
Cloisonné Jewelry with 24K Wires - *Rae* 105
Electroformed Vessels - *Schwarcz* 106
Large Cloisonné On Copper - *Slepian* 107
Layering over Sgraffitoed Liquid Enamel Base Coat - *Stone* 108
Grisaille and Limoges - *Szabados* 109
Risso Screen - *Tanzer* 110
Cloisonné on Steel - *Trippetti* 111
Precious Metal Clay-Silver Enameling - *Vormelker* 112
Liquid Flux as Etching Resist for Bàsse-Taille - *Wallen* 113
Cloisonné Opaque Enamel Jewelry - *Whitney* 114
Selected Pieces from the Collection of Lilyan Bachrach 115

Enameling Techniques (continued)

Foils: Fine Silver and 24K Gold 121
    Marianne Hunter

Decals and Ceramic Pencils 123
    June E. Jasen

Large Mosaic Enamels 127
    Jean Foster Jenkins

Enamel Crayons and Watercolors on Steel and Iron *John Killmaster*	131
Champlevé with Ferric Chloride *Audrey Komrad*	135
Portrait with Enamel Watercolors *Ora K. Kuller*	141
Torch Firing *Deborah Lozier*	145
Vessel Forms *Sarah Perkins*	151
Cloisonné on Fine Silver with 24K Wires *Merry-Lee Rae*	155
Enameling on Electroformed Vessels *June Schwarcz*	159
Large Cloisonné Wall Pieces on Copper *Marian Slepian*	163
Layering over Sgraffitoed Liquid Enamel Base Coat *Judy Stone*	167
Jewelry Size Miniature Paintings *Mona Szabados*	171
Risso Screen *JoAnn Tanzer*	173
Cloisonné on Steel *Joseph Trippetti*	177
Enameling on Fine Silver Metal Clay *Jean Vormelker*	179
Liquid Flux as Etching Resist Bàsse-Taille *Phyllis Wallen*	183
Cloisonné Opaque Enamel Jewelry *Ginny Whitney*	187
Charts	189
Guild and Society Listings	191
Suppliers	197
References	199
Index	201

"It is the most lasting, most beautiful, and most enduring form of decoration—enamel is the eternal art."
— Leonardo Da Vinci

INTRODUCTION

This book has been a long time in coming. I first started writing it in the 1970s when a publisher asked me to write a book on enameling, the craft of fusing glass to metal. I said, "yes" because I wanted to write a book that I could recommend to my students. Well, family matters intervened and I could not take the time to finish the writing. All the notes were stored away until almost two years ago when Jean Jenkins asked me to write a "good" book on enameling because there was not one on the market. I remembered my notes. I had asked a few other professional enamelists to write their methods of working. With each one contributing a text on a different technique, the procedure developed from their practical experience, I knew it would be a better and truer book. I decided to try it again and asked other enamelists to write. The response was wonderful and encouraging.

I am grateful that all the contributors to *Enameling with Professionals* were willing to share what they have learned and made the time to write and revise their texts. They have been very cooperative in answering my many questions about the enamels they use and the details of the way their work. Our intent is to tell you how we enamel in the technique that has been our focus, the technique that we really know, and what works for us. As you will note, there are many ways to enamel. Of course, we agree that there is not one right way. We all think that the way we work today is the best, but we know that tomorrow our method of working could change. Most of us like to experiment and in the field of enameling, there is always something new to try.

The easiest way to learn enameling is to take a hands-on course or even a short workshop. This book is intended to help you understand and learn enameling either by yourself or as a supplement to other instruction.

The first part of the book describes my workshop, with its equipment as a frame of reference, and then gives details about the metals for enameling, the enamel material, some beginner enameling techniques, and suggestions for combining them. Doris

Hall's paisley design is explained because it shows how many different enameling techniques can be combined.

I owe my interest in enameling to Doris Hall, who died in summer 2001. In 1955, I was oil painting and studying silversmithing when I helped form an enameling workshop with nine other women. We called our group Lenox Enamelers. (It survived for five years.) That year, Doris Hall offered an enameling demonstration course and five of us traveled from Worcester, Massachusetts to her Boston studio once a week. She and her husband, Kalman Kubinyi, worked together producing enamels and commissions. After each lesson we would practice in our studio during the week. At the end of the course, Doris gave me the 6" paisley plate she had made to demonstrate. She also gave us this advice: "You may copy this to learn, but do not sign your name to the piece you make because you did not design it." The advice is still good.

Doris taught herself to enamel and enameled as a painter. For her enamel paintings, she treated her copper piece as a canvas and drew in a dried layer of opalescent crackle to produce an oxidized line, a technique she originated. When the opalescent crackle as a base coat was fired high it looked like a flux base coat. She had had Ferro Corporation make her the opalescent crackle. Her painting was developed with the sifters Kalman made for her. His sifters were made with a wire holding a piece of screen and a shaped wooden handle to a plastic tube. We adapted that design by fusing the screen to a plastic tube and cementing on a handle. I am still using most of those sifters.

The color illustrations show the enamel work of all the enamelists who are sharing their studio methods.

The second part of the book is what you would learn if you were fortunate enough to enroll in workshops with all of these professional enamelists. The intent is to show you how to enamel, not what to make. Although an enamel piece can be produced without any knowledge of art, for an enamel to be a work of art depends on the craftsman's ability as an artist in design, drawing, painting, or graphics. All of these can come into play with enamels. I had been enameling for ten years before I enrolled in the fine arts program of art school.

Yes, enameling is truly the art of the fire. It needs the heat of a kiln or a torch to fuse a layer of vitreous enamel to the metal. Unlike ceramics, the enamel work is fired for only a few minutes and then removed to cool. Additional layers of enamel are applied and fired. It is thrilling to watch an enamel piece, after it is removed from the kiln, change color and reveal itself as it cools. The reds, when first taken from a kiln, look brown and slowly become their red as the piece cools. Some opaque enamels fired high become transparents and when refired at a lower temperature are changed back to opaque. We love enamels for their color, brilliance, tactile quality, and the surprises the kiln can give us. We hope that you will find the same delight and pleasure in this wonderful medium, even from your first piece of enamel. Or, if you have this book for the information it offers, we know it will increase your understanding and appreciation of the art of enameling.

Lilyan Bachrach
March 14, 2002

The Enamelist's Vocabulary

Each medium has its own vocabulary and so it is with enamels and enameling. The glass glaze material that is fused to the metal is **enamel**, the finished work is an **enamel piece** and the process is **enameling**. In other words, you enamel an enamel with enamel.

An enamel is **fired** when it is placed in a hot kiln. An electric **kiln** (oven, furnace) is usually used to fuse a **coat** (layer) of enamel to the metal. The pyrometer with the kiln shows the temperature inside the kiln in Fahrenheit (F) or in Centigrade (C). The inside of the kiln is called a **muffle** or **chamber**. The support for transporting the enamel piece in and out of the kiln is a **planche** (firing rack). The tool for lifting the planche is usually a **fork**. A **trivet** or a **hammock** supports an enamel piece by its edges. A **stilt** supports a piece on points in the kiln.

The first layer of enamel on the front and back is a **base coat**. An underfired coat is at the **orange peel stage**. The glossy stage is **at maturity**. **Flash firing** or **healthy firing** is a short, hot firing to quickly gloss the enamel. The size of the enamel grains is the **mesh**. 80 mesh, which is the standard, means that it will sift through a screen that has 80 holes per linear inch. The **fines** are what sifts through after the enamel is sifted through a 325 mesh screen. The enamel material is formulated for firing **soft**, **medium** or **hard**, which refers to the softening point of the enamel. The hardest enamels take the longest to fire to maturity. Methods of applying enamel include **sifting**, **spraying**, **wet packing** (inlaying) and **Indian sand painting**.

To **gum** the piece means to apply an adhesive either to the metal or to the enamel. To **anneal** the metal means to heat it just to the softening point. **Flux** is the colorless, transparent enamel. However, to a jeweler it is a firescale inhibitor that prevents oxidation in soldering. Transparent enamels look differently unfired from when they are fired. The flux, fired on copper, has a golden look. Unfired it looks white, and over a fired enamel it is colorless. New students used to call it "the white stuff", but it is not in our vocabulary.

The Firing Area — Kiln is a #169 Norman Kiln with a 16"x16"x9" chamber. The door supports broke and could not be replaced; the door now opens from the right to left. Pyrometer is on the top right-hand corner to allow for the full use of the kiln top for drying. Two infinite switches, one for each element.

Work table, at right angle to the kiln, is the same height as the inside floor of the kiln. The table is covered with a sheet of ¼" asbestos that was cut to measure. (May no longer be sold) There are two squares of marble, a square of carborundum and a 14"x14"x ⅜" steel plate with the same size steel weight with a handle standing against the wall.

The firing fork has a domed hand protector. The plate on the hammock was fired backside up with the counter enamel on it. The wooden handled stiff spatula is used as a left hand when moving hot pieces with the fork.

The weight was made by a blacksmith. The additional wooden handle was added to eliminate the need for wearing an asbestos glove because the weight absorbs the height from the metal. The weight is used to correct any warpage.

The plate in the foreground has just had a first firing of enamel. The three-pointed stilt that supported it on a planche in the firing, is removed easily when the piece is cool.

The white wire mesh hanging on the wall is a planche that was coated with kiln wash to cover the drips of enamel which could not be removed.

Photo by Bill Byers

Enameling Workshop

Enameling is the process of fusing glass to metal. A layer of glass is applied to a piece of metal; both are heated until the glass wets the metal, flows or spreads out to form a smooth glossy surface, and forms a chemical bond at the interface, at which time the composite is removed from the heat and allowed to cool. That is about all anyone can say about the process. The rest is about procedures and techniques: how to prepare the metal, and the enamel, how to apply the layer of enamel, etc. There are various procedures to accomplish any one of these things.

Enameling begins with cleaning a piece of metal such as copper or fine silver, which are the easiest to enamel. You may wash or screen an enamel to remove the fines. The base coats of enamel are the first layer of enamel on the front and on the back of a piece. Enamels may be applied by sifting, wet packing, spraying or with the thumb and index finger. Spraying is covered by other enamelists elsewhere in this book. You apply a base coat of enamel to the metal piece, fire it, and let it cool. Then you repeat applying and firing additional coats of enamel, which may be from three to thirty or more. The number of layers depends on the design and the technique. The finished enamel piece is either framed or the exposed metal is polished.

Before you purchase equipment and supplies for enameling, you need to decide: what you will make, what will be the largest size piece, what technique you will use, and how many duplicates you want to make. For the beginner, about an 8" electric kiln on a 110V line is probably the most versatile. The size of the kiln determines how large each enamel piece can be. It is best to have at least a one inch margin for the largest piece inside the kiln because the heat is hotter nearer the wires. You can also buy a hot plate kiln or make one with a solid surface hot plate and a small Pyrex pot with a handle to use upside down as a cover. The hot plate kiln used to be a Trinket Kiln. A setup can be made for a torch. Kenneth Bates, in *Enameling: Principles & Practice* (1951), shows a kiln made from metal coffee cans. Deborah Lozier and Edward J. Friedman explain in this book how they use a torch.

The equipment you purchase, based on the decisions you make, determine the workshop space you need. The ideal workshop has a separate area for each function: grinding and buffing metal, sink washing with a work table, firing, enameling, hand finishing and packaging. I am describing my workshop because it is more than adequate. Charles Jeffery said he made his cloisonné jewelry with a kiln on a desk in his bedroom.

When I began enameling, I used our small pantry, which had a sink. After three years with my 110V 8" kiln that had a pyrometer, I graduated to the basement and eventually to my 16" kiln on a 220V line with a door that now opens from right to left. My favorite kiln had a door that opened up. The 16" kiln was re-bricked about ten years ago with 2300 brick. The 2300 brick will withstand a temperature up to 2300°F. The kiln has a

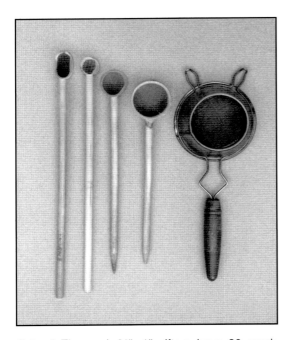

(l. to r.) The oval, ¾", 1" sifters have 80 mesh screen. The ½" sifter has 40 mesh and the old fashioned strainer has a 2" 60 mesh screen. These are but a few of my sifters. When I was doing some six-foot panels, I made sifters from plastic, pint sized measuring cups with handles, just had to cut out the bottom of the cup before melting on the 60 mesh screen. Photo by J.A. Perry

pyrometer in the right hand back corner of the top. It is good to have a spare set of wires for the kiln. Kiln dimensions are usually given width x depth x height. If only one dimension is given, it is for a square floor inside the kiln. The floor of the kiln is protected from enamel drippings with four 6" x 6" x ¼" bisqued ceramic tiles that have been coated with kiln wash. The kiln wash comes in powder form and is mixed with water to a thick paint. I coat about eight of them with a 2" wide inexpensive brush and let them dry overnight. I purchased a box of 25 and foolishly did not coat them first with the kiln wash. There are now other items to protect the kiln floor. Any enamel

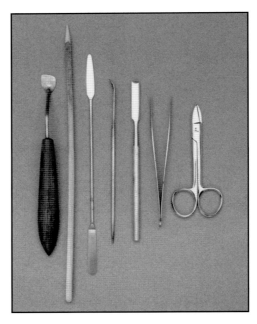

(l. to r.) Painter's spatula with broken tip, sharpened chopstick, dental tools: flexible ends, one end is a narrow scoop with the other end a point and stiff spatula, tweezers with tips slightly filed to dull the tips, straight bezel shears. Photo by J.A. Perry

on the kiln floor will get soft every time you fire the kiln and the feet of the planche will stick to it. Many enamelists vacuum the inside of the kiln because the 2300 brick is apt to shed.

The kiln wires move. They expand as they heat up and contract as they cool. My kiln has the exposed wires sunk in four rows of slots around three sides. If the kiln overheats, a part of the wires could expand and move up and out of its slot. You should push the wire back into its slot only while it is hot, but with the kiln turned off, as the wires become brittle over time. I always wear a cotton smock with long sleeves or a long sleeve cotton shirt with an apron in the workshop. When I have

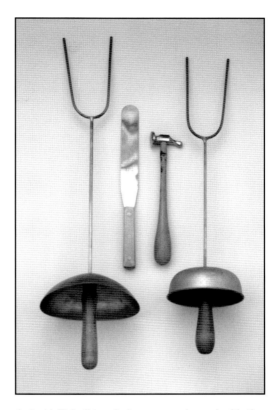

(r. to l.) This firing fork was purchased with the hand guard. The flat end of a chasing hammer is used to help restore form to a warped piece. The stiff blade, wooden handled spatula is the left hand to help support a hot enameled piece as it is moved. This firing fork was made with an 8" bowl for a guard and longer rod for the longer tines. Photo by J.A. Perry

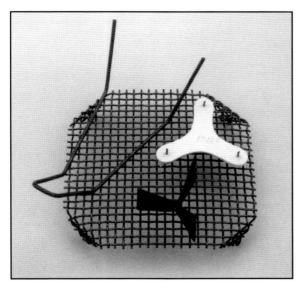

These are firing supports. The hammock, ceramic stilt and the trivet are shown on a 6" square, nichrome mesh planche. The hammock supports a flat piece or an upside down plate or bowl. The stilt supports a piece right side up. This small trivet supports a piece of jewelry on the edges of the jewelry piece. They all come in various sizes and are placed supporting the piece on the planche to be placed in the kiln. Photo by J.A. Perry

received new wires for one of my kilns, I make certain they are labeled for the proper kiln before I store them. They are coiled, but need to be stretched to fit the kiln. There is a formula for the length of wire needed. The man who would rewire my 169 kiln wrapped a piece of leather around one end of a wire and placed that end in a heavy vise. He made a mark in the floor across the room for the vise and stretched the wire to that mark.

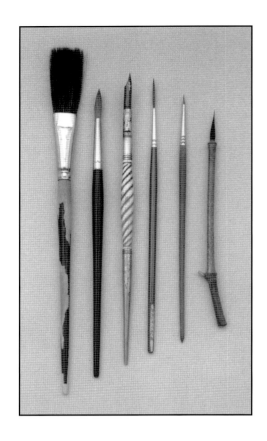

(l. to r.) 1" Greyhound, #3 sable, Hunt 101 nib in pen holder, #1 sable liner, 00 sable, and handmade Lebezon kolinsky watercolor brushes. Photo by J.A. Perry

To purchase replacement wires for your kiln, in addition to the make and model number, you need to know volts, amps, inside kiln measurements, the number of elements and the kind of switch or switches. They come hi-lo-med and infinite. Most potters I know rewire their own kilns.

If you visited my studio this is what you would see. My 16" kiln was purchased with a metal stand that has a shelf near the bottom. I keep the firing forks and asbestos gloves there. Because the metal casing of my kiln gets hot, it is 8" away from the wall and at right angles to a 6-foot sideboard that has a fireproof covering. On top of the sideboard is an assortment of squares: a 12" square x 1" marble slab, a ceramic kiln shelf, and two 3/8" thick steel 14" square plates. To the right of the sideboard is another table with old irons and two heavy weights I had made. On the wall above the sideboard are various sized hammocks I use for firing a plate upside down or a flat piece by opposite edges. To the left of the kiln is a table with a large stainless steel stove protector pad on it for pieces ready to be fired. I usually enamel in a production style for the base coats, which I will explain in my section on overglaze direct painting.

For firing equipment, I have 6" square nichrome mesh planches with the four corners bent down and two 6" x 12" ones with two sides bent down. The planches are now available in stainless steel mesh. My firing forks have a guard for the hand so I do not need to wear a glove when firing. For firing a piece right side up, I use a three-pronged Atlas ceramic stilt or a wire one. When I could not find any more of the ceramic ones, I bought all sizes in four-pronged metal wire stilts. I cut off one prong and bent the stilt to form a triangle. The three points balance better than four points. The other tool is a wooden-handled spatula with about a 10" stiff blade. The spatula is my left hand when I remove the hot enamel from the planche. There is one beside each of the two planche setups for production firing. The double set-tub, with a mixing faucet, has a salad cutting board suspended across one tub. The board is convenient for cloisonné pieces to be stoned under slowly running water and also for scrubbing six switch plates with Penny-Brite® copper cleaner. To the right of the sink is a table with a dish strainer and across from the sink is a 5' table for brushing black crackle (now called liquid form enamel) as a base coat on the backs. Spaced on the table are glass jars to support the pieces when the crackle is applied to the backs and a container for the large brush, a sharpened chopstick, and an iced tea spoon. The brush is to apply the crackle, the spoon is to stir the crackle, and the chopstick to sgraffito my name in the center back of each plate or bowl after the crackle coat dries.

The grinding and polishing equipment are connected to a large dust collector that I bought from a dental supply company. I have two belt sanders: one takes a 1" x 36" fine emery cloth belt and the other a 6" x 48" belt. I use the wider belt sander to bevel the front edge of plates. To use with buffs for cleaning and polishing, I have one motor with two regular sized spindles and one motor with a 10" long spindle that a friend made for me to simplify cleaning the inside of bowls. I have another homemade setup of an electric drill that holds a 5" emery fine disk for sanding the back edge of plates. My friend used an old washing machine motor for that one.

For cutting, there is a Beverly shears and a large vise that will hold a pair of airplane shears. I also have my jeweler's bench with the typical equipment for jeweling and soldering. A six-foot table for sifting or wet packing enamels holds sifters, brushes, pens, bottles of enamels for base coats and a supply of white typing paper. I use white paper under the piece when I am sifting so I can see that the enamel has no unwanted specks. A smaller table holds petri dishes with the overglazes for painting. Two closed closets hold the bottled enamel supply.

Karat Gold Alloys
Stuart Grice, Mill Products Director, Hoover & Strong Inc.

Karat gold alloys fall into several different categories or "marks". In the United States these are 10kt, 14kt, 18kt and 22kt, with Europe having 8kt and 9kt, the Middle East 21kt and the Far East 24kt. A "karat" gold is not pure gold, but an alloy that contains 24th fractions of gold by weight.

10kt	10/24 gold	41.67% gold	18kt	18/24 gold	75.00% gold
14kt	14/24 gold	58.33% gold	22kt	22/24 gold	91.67% gold

Karat gold alloys are commercially available in numerous colors and hues. The most common colors are yellow and white, with pink, red and green becoming popular with fashion trends. The majority of higher karat yellow, pink, red, and green alloys are comprised of gold, silver, and copper. The ratios of each metal can be varied to achieve the different colors. Alloys in the lower karats also contain zinc, generally in quantities up to 10%. Zinc is added for various reasons, but in the lower karats it is a color enhancer and gives yellow alloys a warmer feel. White alloys have are two major sub-families to be considered: gold/nickel and gold/palladium. The palladium alloys do not require the presence of zinc; however, this does not mean zinc will not be present. The nickel alloys usually include zinc up to about 6%. The melting points of typical karat gold alloys are as follows:

10kt Yellow-500°F	14kt Yellow-1500°F	18kt Yellow-1580°F
10kt White-1770°F	14kt White-1800°F	18kt White-1650°F
10kt Red-1715°F	14kt Red-1700°F	18kt Red-1630°F
10kt Green-1530°F	14kt Green-1600°F	18kt Green-1780°F
	22kt Yellow-1830°F	

Enameling fine gold has an obvious advantage: gold does not oxidize under normal circumstances. When considering the alloys of gold, oxidation of base metal additions in the alloys (copper, zinc, nickel, cadmium, tin and indium) makes life somewhat harder. The piece must be heated to bring the base metals to the surface and to oxidize them. Then follow several warm picklings, acid baths usually about 75°F. Most jewelers put their pickle in a small electric crock pot.

The first pickle, usually sulfuric, removes the oxides of base metals; i.e., they revert from oxides to base metals. The second pickle, nitric, removes the base metals themselves, but also silver, which is not a base metal. These metals migrate to the surface, but they can only travel a certain distance, and oxidation will only occur to a certain depth below the surface. Therefore, the process must be repeated several times. After the last nitric solution pickle, a fine gold layer is on the surface. Not all the base metals have been removed; the majority remain below the surface.

Copper oxide prevents enamel adhesion and also results in color problems, but by far the most inconvenient addition for enameling is zinc. Not only does zinc oxide prevent adhesion and lead to color problems, but also it will be released from the metal surface as a vapor at enameling temperatures. These problems will occur even if the surface has been pre-cleaned and lead to unavoidable problems once the enamel layer is in place.

Consequently, the best karat gold alloys for enameling are either zinc-free or contain very low zinc concentrations, typically 2% or less. As a metallurgical purist, I say 1% zinc. Alloys containing higher levels can be enameled, but more care is necessary in the preparation stages. All work pieces must be depletion gilded, sometimes known as fire gilding, before the first layer of enamel is applied. In this process, the work piece is annealed without a fire coat protection to allow the base metal — usually copper, zinc and sometimes nickel if white gold alloys are used — to oxidize. Sometimes quenching the work piece into water once the red glow has disappeared helps; but be careful of this step if using a 14kt or 18kt nickel white alloy since cracking can occur when quenching. The oxides are then removed in an acid pickle bath of 10% sulfuric, followed by base metal removal by further pickling in 10% nitric acid. A caution: if you leave the work piece in too long, all the base metal will be removed and the work piece will disintegrate. The various pickle baths will leave a fine gold enriched surface. The pickling process must be repeated several times to ensure all the base metals are removed from the surface. As a general rule, the lower the karat, the more repetitions since a higher content of base metals is present.

It is wise to note at this point that problems can occur when enameling high karat red gold alloys. With 10kt red alloys only the oxide issue requires consideration, while for 14kt, and in particular 18kt red gold alloys, things can be a little different. Internal strains occur on cooling from annealing temperatures because of atomic movement. These factors make the metals hard and can also distort the work piece, and in extreme cases cracking can occur. Quenching from above 770°F will reduce these possibilities, but not once the first coat of enamel has been applied. 18kt red alloys are probably the most difficult to enamel successfully.

As a general rule, when choosing a karat gold alloy for enameling, the higher the karat the better, since as the karat level goes down, the base metal content goes up, particularly for zinc. Yellow alloys are usually easier to enamel than whites and reds. All karat gold can be enameled with transparent enamels. If sufficient depletion gilding has been done, there is no need to fire a layer of opaque enamel; fuse fine gold over this opaque layer and then transparent enamel to finish. The fine gold layer resulting from the depletion gilding means that transparent enamels can be fired directly onto the work piece. The less the base metal additions in the alloy, the easier the process will be and the less potential for failure there is. Most 18kt yellow alloys have little or no zinc present and are therefore the best alloys to use. Problems can occur when using opaque red, green and yellow enamels, which tend to discolor to brown if overheated.

When ordering karat gold alloys for enameling, ask about zinc content and what is recommended as the best alloy in the karat range you can afford. Most metal suppliers do not carry specialized enameling karat gold alloys, so cost should be no different from standard alloys. At Hoover & Strong, the minimum weight order for sheet is 2 dwts for gold, in any karat or color. As a guide, a 1" square sheet in 20 ga will weigh approximately 5 dwts in 18kt yellow, 4.4 dwts in 14kt yellow and 3.9 dwts in 10kt yellow. For 22 ga sheet, these weights become 4 dwts, 3.5 dwts and 3 wts respectively.

Enameling techniques and considerations required for base metals also apply when using karat gold alloys.

- Make sure all soldering operations have been completed with a suitable grade solder, i.e., with a melt point greater than the enameling temperature. Always keep solder joints to a minimum since karat gold solders often contain zinc and also cadmium, which behaves like zinc when heated and will have similar associated problems.

- It is usual to heat treat the work piece prior to enameling in order to relieve any residual stress present. The preheating will prevent distortion that may otherwise occur during the enameling firing cycle. This can be done at a low temperature, around 660°F, for a minute or two before the depletion gilding process. Most enamellers will depletion gild 3-4 times to ensure no base metals remain in the surface. This will also totally stress relieve the work piece and ensure that no distortion occurs. The actual number of times required will become an "experience" thing for each enameller, who will become comfortable with a particular suppliers product. Four depletion gilds should be the maximum required under most circumstances. Better too many than too few.

- After the final depletion gild, the work piece must be meticulously cleaned. Traditionally this takes place by pickling in warm 10% nitric acid to remove any traces of oxides, grease and dirt. Some enamellers prefer to use 10% sulfuric acid since it is less reactive and will produce a suitably clean surface. Nitric acid will result in a superior surface, if required.

- Either method requires neutralizing the piece in an alkali bath such as 10% sodium bicarbonate to remove any traces of pickling acid. Ideally do this in an ultrasonic bath. Any entrapped acids remaining in surface porosity or areas where liquids may become entrapped by capillary action will eventually result in corrosion products and will lead to discoloration.

- An alternative cleaning method, which is increasing in popularity, is electrolytic stripping. This provides an excellent surface finish for enameling, but equipment costs have to be considered.

Typical problems when enameling karat gold alloys:

- Poor enamel adhesion due to an inadequately cleaned surface.

- Poor enamel adhesion due to the presence of oxides at the surface of the work piece. The oxides are usually from copper, zinc or nickel.

- Enamel discoloration as a result of oxides at the surface of the work piece.

- Enamel discoloration resulting from entrapped pickling acids in either surface porosity or areas where residues may be retained by capillary action. The entrapped acids will result in the generation of corrosion products, which can be seen through transparent enamel. If a work piece or component has been investment cast the probability of porosity at the surface is greatly increased for shrinkage and gas porosity are known defects from this manufacturing method.

- Work piece failure due to assembly using a solder of insufficiently high melt point.

- Partial liquation of the work piece due to the melt point of the alloy being exceeded in the enameling process.

In summary, when choosing gold alloys for enameling, use a zinc-free or low zinc alloy if possible. Be aware of the increased potential for copper oxidation and distortion, particularly in 18kt, from red alloys. It is not intended to suggest that these alloys cannot be enameled, only that they need to be treated with respect and great care.

REFERENCES:
S. Grice, "But I've Always Done It this Way. Technical Support — It Makes A Difference." 12th Santa Fe Symposium On Jewelry Manufacturing Technology, 1998. Met-Chem Research Inc.

"Jewellery Enamels And Their Applications To Copper Based Metals." Johnson Matthey Blythe Colors Data Sheet C17.

W. S. Rapson and T. Groenewald, *Gold Usage*, Academic Press, 1978.

Stuart Grice is the Mill Products Director at Hoover & Strong Inc., VA. Previous positions: Metallurgical manager, Cookson Precious Metals Ltd., Birmingham, England. Senior Metallurgist, Johnson Matthey Jewellery Ltd., Birmingham, England. Higher National Diploma in applied Physics HND). Materials Science (BSc). Representative, British Jewellers Association, on the International Standards Technical Committee STI/53, 1997-2000.

METALS FOR ENAMELING

COPPER

The most commonly used metals for enameling are pure copper and fine silver. The fine silver is primarily used for jewelry because of its cost, color and the advantage of not producing a firescale coat like copper does when it is fired. The copper is the most used metal for enameling for many reasons: its malleability, its color, availability, and cost. In addition, it usually maintains its shape in the firing process. The appropriate gauge (thickness) of the metal depends on what is being made. Most plates and vessels are usually 18 ga while jewelry can range from 28 ga for a repoussé piece to 14 ga for champlevé. The smaller the gauge number, the thicker the metal. If pure copper is to be ordered from a mill, it is necessary to specify the form, such as sheet, wire, etc., the gauge and the end use (enamel on copper). The *Thompson Enamel Workbook* specifications are "oxygen free, high conductivity copper, conforming to ASTM specifications B-170." I do use the 20 ga sheet copper from a plumbing supply company for pieces up to 4"x10" with about five firings and I have not had any problems. I have not used it for more firings because the need has not arisen.

BASE COATED STEEL

I have used steel in flat 12" squares that came with their undercoat and base coat already fired. If I overfired them so that they warped, it sometimes was impossible to flatten them even though they were fired and weighted many times to try to correct the warping. Copper is more forgiving if it becomes warped. Steel needs a special undercoat before the base coat is applied. Purchased with the base coats, the pieces only need to be degreased with a detergent before enameling.

FINE SILVER

I usually dome jewelry that I fabricate of 26 ga or 28 ga fine silver or oxygen-free copper. Doming the thin gauge metal gives it added strength and keeps the piece of jewelry, especially pins, from being too heavy. I often leave the 18 ga and 20 ga fine silver flat. I do counter enamel all of my enamels. Many enamelists say that there is less probability of the enamel cracking if the base coats have the same enamel.

CLOISONNÉ WIRE

I like to purchase both fine silver and fine gold cloisonné wire that is not annealed because it is easier to make a straight line with the wire stiff and it is easy to anneal it for intricate lines. To anneal the wire, loosely and carefully wind it into a three to four inch roll and fire. To test whether the wire is annealed when you take it out of the kiln, bend back one end; if it stays bent, it is annealed and if it does not, it needs additional firing.

FOILS

The only foils I have used are the standard 24K gold and fine silver and also a heavier fine silver foil known as "clutch" silver. Although many enamelists pierce the foil, I never do, even though I have used the full 3" square sheets on enameled pieces. Jean Jenkins places the foil, after she cuts it, on an anti-static sheet. I cut a sheet of foil between two pieces of tracing paper with various sized sharp scissors. I have a 10" pair that I use for long diagonal cuts. The foil is placed on the enameled piece with a water-dampened #1 liner brush. Additional water is added to the piece if the foil needs to be repositioned. The water is drawn off with a paper towel by pressing down on the towel. If the foil does not adhere to the enamel surface after the water dries, then add at 1:2 diluted gum and wait until it dries to fire the piece. For the first firing of the foil, I often sift about a ¼" circle of soft flux on an area that has no foil. This spot of flux will tell me when the foil is fused. If you overfire the foil in the first firing, you will destroy it. After the first firing, I smooth the foil with a glass brush. The foil can be fired higher after there are two layers of transparents over it.

CLEANING COPPER BY BUFFING WHEEL

If you use primarily transparent enamels, any marks on the metal surface will show. A bright surface enhances the brilliance of transparent enamels. To achieve the surface on copper, I use the buffing wheel. **Caution:** Although I have an exhaust system, I wear a nose mask, a face mask, a shower cap and cotton or leather gloves. To be safe, you need to know how to use the equipment.

I use a 5" cotton goblet buff charged with Lea Compound C, a greaseless compound for copper in a metal tube. Cut off about 2" of the tube, remove the wrapping, and place the piece of compound in a small glass jar with just enough water to cover the compound. The jar needs to be tall enough for you to stir the compound after it is soft. Left overnight, the compound absorbs the water and is soft enough to be stirred into a smooth paste. I apply a thick coat of the compound paste to the goblet buff mounted on the spindle of the buffing wheel. A stiff, small, metal spatula works well for spreading the compound on the buff. I usually let it dry overnight to a hard, crusty state. I soften the cutting action of the buff by first giving a few swipes with a piece of scrap copper across the spinning charged buff. You can clean over twelve 6" pieces before the buff needs to be recharged.

You can also apply the Lea Compound C directly to a buff on a spinning spindle at 1725 rpm by holding the open end of the compound tube again the buff. This thin coating on the buff will dry within five minutes and then you can buff the piece. Charged this way, the buff will need to be recharged with the compound after a few pieces.

I buff the front of the piece first and the back second. By buffing the front first, the finger marks on the back will be removed when you hold the piece by the edge to buff the back of the piece. If it is difficult to hold the piece by its edge, I wear clean white cotton gloves to buff the second side.

Materials for cleaning copper with a buffing wheel and Lea Compound C: (shown up and around from the left) new 3" goblet buff; 5" goblet buff coated with Lea Compound C; open tupe of compound stored in metal frozen juice can; new tube of Lea Compound C; glass jar of compound paste; table knife to apply paste to buff; new 6" x 1" cotton muslin buff.   Photo by Bill Byers

The Lea Compound C is stored with the cut end standing tightly inside a small, metal, frozen juice can with a wet paper towel in the bottom to prevent the compound from drying out.

CLEANING COPPER IN AN ACID BATH

The first rule for using acids is **ADD ACID TO WATER, NOT WATER TO ACID**. The most commonly used acids for removing firescale from copper, sterling, and gold alloys are commercial grade nitric acid and Sparex 2, an acid-type cleaning compound in granular form. Acid diluted in water is called a "pickle." Jewelers often say, "pickle it." The solution can be used in a hard rubber photography tray, a Pyrex

Charging a new 5" x 1" muslin buff with Lea Compound C paste. The spindle was custom made the extra long length to accommodate buffing the inside of deep bowls with a goblet buff.   Photo by Bill Byers

container, or an electric slow cooker. The pickle works best when warm, but it should not be allowed to boil.

Although Sparex 2 is considered a "safe" acid, both the nitric acid solution and the Sparex 2 will eat holes in fabric. The weaker the solution, the slower the biting action. The recommended solution for the Sparex 2 is 10 ounces by weight in warm water to make a quart of solution. I have only used the Sparex 2 in the electric slow cooker after soldering silver or gold jewelry. I do not clean the copper with acid, but other enamelists explain how they use it and dispose of the acid.

The other rule when using an acid bath is **use wooden or copper tongs. Tongs made of iron will contaminate the acid bath**. If a deep container is used for the acid bath, wear special, long, heavy rubber gloves when you reach into the tank.

CLEANING COPPER BY HAND

Each enamelist has a preferred product for cleaning copper. Among the ones I have used are a liquid dish detergent, a rag soaked in vinegar and dipped in salt, and a scouring powder with a scouring pad. I prefer Penny-Brite. I have used it for over twenty years. It is a copper cleaner with the right ph. I place a number of small pieces, or one 12" plate, on the wooden board across the top of a set tub. This board for cutting vegetables at the sink, is sold in kitchen supply stores. I rub one side of all the pieces with a scouring pad and Penny-Brite, then turn them over, clean the other side, and rinse them well. The piece is grease-free if the water sheets off (does not bead). Sometimes I wear rubber gloves. I place each piece in the dish strainer, dry them with a cotton towel, and if I am not coating the backs with liquid black enamel at the time,

I wrap each piece in paper. If I am ready to brush on the crackle, I place each piece, back side up, on a bottle on the nearby table. *(see page 45)*

If the water, gum, or crackle pulls apart (coagulates) while you brush it on, you can clean the spot with a little enamel, crackle, or saliva to remove the grease from that small area.

CLEANING FINE SILVER

I clean fine silver in the kiln. I first put a number of fine silver, jewelry size pieces, on trivets into a 1500°F kiln to remove any grease or discoloration. I peek into the kiln to check whether they are clean. Fine silver is silvery white when clean. When the pieces are cool, I rub one piece at a time with 000 steel wool. A piece is placed on a small sheet of typing paper, and one corner of the paper is turned over a small part of the piece to keep the oil from my finger off the metal. My finger keeps the piece from moving. I rub in one direction over the face of the piece, usually from top to bottom. The clean pieces are placed face side down on a clean sheet of paper about 2" apart for a base coat of very thin crackle. I use the fine silver for cloisonné pins and pendants.

The Manufacture of Enamels
Woodrow Carpenter

Minerals such as silica, soda ash, potassium nitrate, borax, calcium carbonate, etc. are weighed according to each enamel formula, well mixed, and loaded into a preheated fire clay crucible. The batch is heated to a selected temperature for a sufficient length of time to melt the minerals, forming a viscous liquid, and continued until all gases released during the decomposition of the minerals are eliminated. The enamel is removed by ladling or pouring it onto a thick iron plate where it cools to form "cake" or "lump," into water where it is shattered to be called "frit," or through water cooled iron rolls to be called "roll quenched." The cake and roll quenched are also known as air cooled. The minerals mentioned above will produce colorless transparent enamels. Changing the proportions of these minerals will provide a wide range of firing temperatures and thermal expansions, as well as small changes in gloss, surface tension, and other properties less well known.

Other minerals may be included in the colorless transparent enamel formula. Some crystalline minerals have a low solubility in glass. These insoluble crystals will decrease the transparency. Depending on their size, number, and index of refraction, the decrease can range from a slight cloudiness to a dense opaque white. This range of opacity has been described in terms such as translucent, opal, opalescent, and opaque.

Several manmade ceramic pigments are added to control color. When added in the absence of insoluble crystals, the result is a transparent color, frequently called translucent. When insoluble crystals are present, the result is an opaque color.

LEAD FREE AND LEAD BEARING ENAMELS

The composition of lead and lead-free enamels differ only in that the former may contain as much as fifty percent lead while the latter contains no lead. Any change in an enamel's composition may require some change in the procedures used by the artist who wishes to obtain the same end results. Different enamel compositions have different optimum firing ranges to produce their best visual properties such as gloss, clarity, and smoothness. This firing range is rather narrow, usually a spread of 30-50°F, and a length of time AT THAT temperature, which must be determined by the artist.

Furnaces that are slow coming back to temperature after inserting the piece may require a total of 5 minutes or more to provide the proper length of time at the optimum temperature. Artists who fire by observing the surface of the piece, with little regard to what their indicating pyrometer reads, have had no trouble firing lead-free enamels. Artists who arbitrarily fire at what they think their indicating pyrometer should read, and at a predetermined time, have problems switching from one enamel to another even if both are lead enamels.

I cannot tell you what your pyrometer should read or how long you should fire to obtain a clear flux coating of lead-free enamel on copper. I can tell you that in my furnace with my controlling pyrometer set at 1500°F the length of firing is four minutes. If you can arrive at a comparable fire, the result will be equal to or better than any lead-bearing enamel. When using opaque lead-free I set my controlling pyrometer at 1500°F and fire for three minutes. Using a controlling pyrometer eliminates the need to look at the enamel while in the furnace once you determine the optimum fire (temperature and time).

We know many artists who feel their lead-free transparent colors are superior to lead-bearing enamels. On the other hand, many feel lead-bearing opaques have a little more gloss, but they continue to use unleaded for health reasons.

Lead enamels can be fired as a subsequent coat over lead-free enamels; lead-free enamels can be fired as a subsequent coat over most lead enamels. They can be sandwiched. For example: a lead flux, lead-free color, followed by a lead color. Again, the secret is in the firing. All of this was done quite extensively in the sixteenth century in Limoges. Prior to that, the eleventh century champlevé enamels by the Limoges and Mosan masters were lead-bearing white, yellow, and green, while all other colors were lead-free.

There is one caution. As mentioned above, a complete coat of lead enamel can be applied over a fired coat of lead-free, however, if only one or two grains of lead enamel falls onto a lead-free surface and fired, a pit will result. Thompson stopped making lead enamels because of OSHA's workplace restrictions on the airborne lead.

Woodrow Carpenter, owner of Thompson Enamel, Inc., fired his first enamel in 1935. In 1950, he began manufacturing and selling enamel colors. In 1981, he purchased the Thomas C. Thompson Company. In 1982, he began publishing *Glass on Metal*, which is now the publication of The Enamelist Society. He founded the Society in 1986. *Glass on Metal* has many technical articles on the composition and properties of enamels and their firing written by Mr. Carpenter.

The Enamel Material

Enamel comes in a number of forms: lump, string, liquid, and powder, as well as in the optical qualities of transparent, opaque, and opalescent. The important factor in selecting an enamel is that it be made for the metal you are using. Enamel expands as it is fired and then contracts as it cools. This is called thermal expansion. The metal on which the enamel is fired must expand and contract at a slightly higher rate.

Enamels are sold in assorted lump forms and in meshes, probably as coarse as 10 mesh and as fine as #325. Some enamelists use the fines for a painting technique. I principally use 80 mesh powder, overglazes, and the 20 mesh in transparents for some jewelry.

Enamels are manufactured in soft, medium, and hard fusing, which refers to how they fire. The soft enamels fire the most quickly. Some enamelists refer to the soft enamels as delicate. In Thompson's catalog, most of the 80 mesh enamels for copper, steel, silver, and gold are listed as medium fusing. Only the flux and the black have a listing as soft; the flux has an additional listing for hard.

When I first studied enameling, I was taught to use only the 80 mesh soft flux as the base coat and then the medium fusing enamels for subsequent coats. It was not until I concentrated on painting with overglazes that I changed to using medium fusing enamel as a base coat because it did not bubble up through subsequent layers of enamel. It is now accepted that you first apply the hard firing enamels, then medium over those, and the soft enamels for the top coats.

Some enamelists do not remove the fines from their enamels. To remove the fines from ground enamels, i.e., clean them, you either wash them or screen them through a stack of various mesh screens. To use the screens, you stack them with the coarsest mesh screen on the top and place a penny in each one to help move the enamel. You shake them until the fines are at the bottom. Then you put each screened enamel in a separate labeled container.

To wash the enamels, use either your tap water, depending on its quality, or distilled water. I wash only the enamels I use for jewelry. Place some enamel in a jar, add water, stir, let it start to settle, and pour off the milky substance in the top of the jar. This process is repeated until the water in the jar with the enamel is clear. I seldom wash more than ¼ cup of an enamel at a time and often just a teaspoonful.

An early instructor of mine had a wide-mouth gallon bottle into which we poured the milky substance when we washed the enamels. When enough waste was accumulated, the water at the top was poured off, some fresh water added, stirred, let settle, and the milky water poured off. When dry, this discarded enamel was added to the counter enamel. I spread out the washed enamel on two stacked sheets of clean paper near the back of the kiln top and cover it with another sheet of white paper to keep it clean while it is drying.

Enamels are best stored in bottles with a screw-on lid, labeled with their number, manufacturer and mesh size. If the enamel has been washed, I add that to the label. The labeled bottles, arranged by color and transparent or opaque, are kept in a closed cabinet.

COLOR SAMPLE BOARD

Many enamelists have enamel color sample boards, one for opaques and one for transparents. The opaques only need two siftings of the colors you own. The transparents, often on ½" x 3" of 20 ga or 18 ga copper, show the transparent color on the bare copper, over flux, medium white, silver foil, and gold foil. You have to divide each piece into five sections: the top fifth is for the transparent on the copper. You can either coat that section with Scalex or leave it uncoated

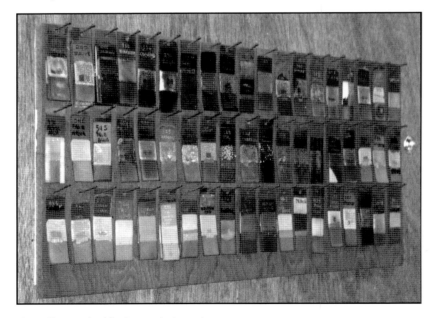

Jean Foster Jenkins' sample board.

to clean after the first firing. The next section down is 80 mesh medium flux, the third one down is medium fusing white, and the last two sections are for the silver and gold foil. The sections under the foil can be the flux or the white enamel. Fire the samples' base coats and then fire a transparent enamel color over the entire piece.

For fine silver samples, I clean ½" discs in the kiln, brush a thin coat of crackle on the back, and sgraffito an enamel number in the dry crackle. I sift and fire a covering coat of soft flux. Then I sift and fire a covering coat of transparent enamel color. I keep the fine silver samples in a plastic box.

BINDERS (Enameling Gum)

Although enamel can be applied dry, there are many times when you need to mix the enamel with a binder that is an enameling gum adhesive. Years ago, the only adhesives that enamelists were taught to use were gum tragacanth and agar. I remember buying tragacanth flakes, dissolving them in water, and then storing the solution in the refrigerator. When Klyr-Fyre came on the market, I bought a gallon of it because it had an unlimited shelf life. Other enamelists do use CMC (carbo-metho-cellulose). Jean Jenkins gives a recipe for 5 gallons.

APPLYING ENAMELS

Enamels may be applied by sifting, wet packing, spraying or with the thumb and index finger. I do not own a sprayer, but its use is covered in this book by other enamelists.

MAKING A SIFTER

Except for an old fashioned, metal-sided, 2" diameter, flat-screened bottom tea strainer with a wooden handle, I make my own. Other enamelists do, too. My sifters were adapted from the one Kalman Kubinyi made. I cut about a 1" piece of plastic tubing, diameters ranging from ¼" to 1½", and shape one end of a ¼" wooden dowel with a half-round file to fit the tubing. I place a piece of screening, larger than the tube, against a hot electric iron and then press the plastic tube's open end against the screen. The two are held together until I see the plastic melt into the screening. I have an old iron that I keep for this purpose. (Sarah Perkins says that she uses a spatula for fusing the screen and the plastic.) The unit is removed, the screen is trimmed close to the plastic, and then the shaped end of the dowel is attached with Duco cement to the tube. The tube is placed on the workbench with the tube flat on its side and the dowel handle upright and supported against a set of drawers for the cement to dry overnight.

SIFTING

I sift over a stack of two or three sheets of white paper. I use clean white paper to see any speck in the enamel to be removed to keep my enamels clean. The sifter, half filled with an enamel, is on the paper. Students learn to sift an even coat by covering most of the sheet of paper a number of times with counter enamel in a 2" sifter. I sift by tapping on the handle of the sifter with my index finger. If you hold the sifter close to the paper, you limit the spread of the enamel as it falls from the sifter. If you want an overall fine layer, then you hold the sifter up higher and tap it lightly. You have learned to sift the enamel when you can do it without thinking about it.

When you need to wet the metal before sifting on the enamel, you can use an airbrush, a soft brush, or a hand spray bottle. I remember Kenneth Bates telling students in a workshop that you aimed the sprayer at the ceiling and let the solution fall on the piece as the gentle rain from heaven. If you are using a hand spray bottle, set the nozzle to the finest spray and pump it a few times before spraying the metal. If you do not have a spray booth and you are doing a lot of spraying with a gum solution, it is advisable to cover a section of the floor with newspapers. A floor wet with gum solution is very slippery. I do most of my spraying with water so there is no problem with a slippery cement floor.

WET PACKING (Inlaying) 80 or 100 MESH ENAMEL

I pick up damp enamel with the tip of a #1, #2, or #3 sable liner brush and place it in the top left hand area of the design. With the side of the brush, I level the enamel to about 1 mm thick, wipe off the brush, and again with the side of the brush, draw off any excess water. The next damp color is placed almost up to the first color and then the new color is pushed against the first color, evened out, and so it continues. The size of the brush you use depends on the area an enamel color is to cover. You might need to add a very little bit of diluted enameling gum if you are working on a sloping surface. If you are going to wet pack a piece that is larger than 4", you should start in a far corner and progress diagonally down to the opposite corner. That way your hand does not disturb the enamel while you are applying it with the brush. Other enamelists use other tools for wet packing. Just try them all.

INDIAN SAND PAINTING (Thumb and Finger Application)

This techniques takes practice. The space between the first and second joint of your index finger is placed next to some dry 80 mesh enamel on a sheet of paper. (I have not used it with other enamel meshes.) Your thumb slides across the enamel and holds the enamel against the flat area of your index finger. You start releasing the enamel by sliding your thumb forward. You begin either at the top or the bottom of the line you are making.

APPLYING LIQUID FORM ENAMEL (Crackle) AS COUNTER BASE COAT

Although the name of the material has been changed, what I still have and use was called "crackle." The name refers to what happens once this liquid form enamel is applied and fired over a previously fired coat of 80 mesh soft enamel. The liquid form breaks up or cracks in the firing because the soft enamel underneath expands first. I suspect it was a porcelain slip made for pottery. I still call it crackle.

When I last purchased Thompson #772 Black it came in a plastic gallon jug. I poured the liquid into a big basin and cut off the top of the jug to spoon out the mass at the bottom of the jug. After a lot of stirring with a long cooking spoon, I was able to get the material into solution. I divided the crackle into many wide-necked, glass pint jars with screw-on covers, by stirring the crackle before each ladle-full was poured into a jar. The jars were filled to within 1" of the top to leave room for stirring the crackle before using it.

After my course with Doris Hall in 1955, I used the black crackle as the base coat on the back of all my plates, plaques, and shallow bowls. Originally, I held the piece over a bowl and used a

Black crackle (liquid form enamel) is being applied to the back of a cleaned copper plate. The brush is a 1" Greyhound. Although half the length of the well-charged brush is held against the plate, no pressure is being exerted. The liquid enamel is feathered onto the plate. Photo by Bill Byers

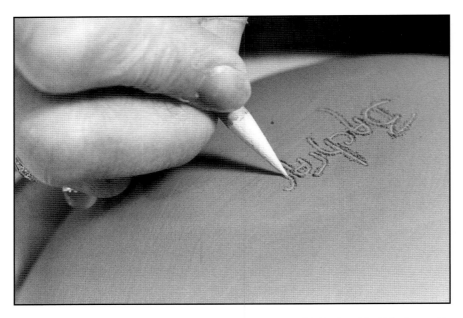

Signature is being sgraffitoed with a sharpened chopstick in the dried black crackle on the back of the plate. The plate will be tapped on its edge to remove the loose dry crackle.   Photo by Bill Byers

small ladle to pour the crackle on the piece. Sometimes I would move the crackle with the convex side of the ladle.

I soon found that it was simpler to use a well-charged, large brush for applying the crackle. I still apply the crackle with a 1" greyhound brush. When you first receive the liquid form enamel, stir it well with a slender spoon and test a brush full. If it is too thick, gradually add a very small amount of water while stirring. Experience will tell you the right consistency. The brushing consistency is a little thicker than the one for pouring. It used to come with a binder, so if I thinned it too much, I would set it aside to evaporate. Now if that happens, I add a little Klyr-Fyre, stir it well, and it thickens. Sometimes I even have to add a little more water. For my undercoat of counter, the crackle does not need to be an absolutely smooth coat because I will cover it with a counter enamel that is mainly opaque enamels. If I needed that smooth a coat, I probably would have bought an airbrush and set up a spray booth.

The piece to be coated with crackle is placed on a jar so it is at least 2" above the table; the side to be coated, usually the back, is facing up. The table is covered with white paper. If I am coating only one piece and the crackle is very thick, I just wet the brush and swish it around the top of the crackle in its jar and then brush it lightly on the cleaned metal piece. When the crackle is dry, I sgraffito my name with a sharp chopstick in the center back of the plate. If the dried crackle powders off on your hand as you hold the piece to sift enamel on the front, it means it does not have sufficient adhesive. You can either bear with it, or remove the dried crackle and recoat the back of the piece. The crackle needs to have about a half teaspoon of Klyr-Fyre stirred into the jar. When applying the crackle with a brush, you pass the brush over the piece as though it were a feather. If you bear down on the brush as you stroke the metal, the crackle will not cover smoothly.

When applying the crackle to a round plate, the last swipes with the brush are around the edge of the plate. When I have finished using the crackle, I wipe around the top of the jar, add a little water and screw on the lid. My old jars have metal lids so I put a piece of white paper over the top before I screw on the lid. The brush and the spoon get a good washing. The brush is used only for the black crackle.

The first sifted layer of enamel on the bare metal, the base coat, is being applied to the front of the plate. The enamel being sifted is 80 mesh flux. The enamel in the sifter covers the bottom of the sifter and fills only half of the sifter. The white enamel in the other sifter, sitting on a sheet of white paper, will be sifted over the flux coat before the piece is fired. The fingers of the supporting hand are under the tray, which has a coat of unfired, dry black crackle. The plate is held tilted to have the enamel fall on the edge. The index finger taps on the sifter to apply the enamel. The excess enamel on the paper is from sifting beyond the edge of the plate and from setting the sifter down to even out the enamel in the bottom of the sifter. The sifter is the old fashioned strainer that has a flat 60 mesh screen on the bottom. Photo by Bill Byers

THE FIRING PROCESS

If my electric kiln had a rheostat, I would set it at 1500°F and be able to forget it until I was ready to fire. I should have installed a rheostat; I do not know why I did not get to it. I now turn on both infinite controls to the highest number and set a timer for 25 minutes as a reminder to check the kiln temperature. If I should forget, and I have, the inside of the kiln is almost white and the wires may be burned out. When the temperature is at 1500°F, I turn the controls down to hold at about 1350°F. The longer the kiln is on, the more heat the bricks absorb and although the pyrometer reads the same 1500°F as it did when it first reached that temperature, it recovers faster. A heat-saturated kiln is preferable.

Everytime you open the kiln door, the temperature drops. If the kiln furniture is cold when you put the piece in the kiln, the temperature will drop even more. Although 1500°F is 1500°F, I think of a kiln that just came to temperature as a cooler kiln than one that has been at that temperature for over an hour. The inside back of the kiln is hotter than the front part, so I often rotate a large piece for the firings. The firing is hotter closer to the wires. For larger pieces I watch that, too, and I am careful to limit their size in order to leave one inch from the wires.

The recovery time of the kiln's temperature is important because when you place an enameled piece in the kiln, the previously fired layer of enamel cracks and mends itself. If the kiln is too cool, the cracks remain.

SIFTING 80 MESH ENAMEL and FIRING FRONT AND BACK BASE COATS

With this method, the front and the back of the enamel is fired in the first firing. If the piece is flat or shallow, I spray water to hold the sifted enamel in place. If the piece is a deep bowl, I spray with diluted 1:3 Klyr-Fyre. Holding the underside of the piece with the dried crackle resting on my fingers, I spray lightly, sift, spray, sift, and spray, applying a damp enamel coat that covers the copper. I use the 2" 60 mesh sifters for the base coats. Three of the 2" 60 mesh sifters are labeled to be used only for flux, white, or for counter. If I have used only water and sprayed lightly, the piece can be fired almost immediately. If I have used enameling gum, the piece has to be dry. If you are in a hurry, you can set the piece, right side up on hot kiln furniture. If the gum is not dry, you will see some steam rise up when you place it in the kiln. Take the piece out of the kiln, wait a few seconds, and then return it to the kiln. You can also put the set up piece in the hot kiln for a second, take it out to check for steam, and then repeat until there is no steam. I fire at 1500°F until the front base coat is smooth. When I remove the piece from the kiln, I check that the crackle on the back is shiny and smooth; if it is not, I quickly put it back in the kiln for additional firing. If the crackle is not fired adequately, it will chip off as the piece cools.

The second firing completes the counter enamel of the back. For my counter, I mix about 1/3 Thompson #124A hard black 80 mesh leaded enamel with 2/3 left over mixed enamels. If one enamel color contaminates another, this mixed enamel (often called tweed) is put in a quart bottle and used for my counter. Two good siftings with the 60 mesh screen sifter are applied over the fired crackle, spraying with water before and after each sifting. The spraying between coats changes the color of the enamel enough to let you see where you have sifted. For the sifting on the back, I hold the plate with the center front of the piece on my fingers so none of my fingers are protruding from under the plate. I start the sifting around the edge, moving the plate in a circular fashion and then sift around towards my signature but not over it. The center back has the signature covered with Thompson #426 leaded 80 mesh soft flux after two coats of counter are sifted on the back.

Sifting on counter enamel. The back of the plate is having counter enamel sifted over the fired base coat of black crackle. The supporting hand and fingers are all underneath the plate. The plate is held with its edge at right angle to the sifter. The oxidized line of the sgraffitoed signature is not covered with the counter enamel. It will be covered with soft flux before the piece is fired. Photo by Bill Byers

Techniques for Beginners

After you learn to apply enamels by sifting, wet packing, brushing on crackle and firing the base coats, you are ready for some of the simple techniques that require only a feel for color. You can design a piece by repeating one technique or learning to combine techniques. If you are enameling samples of the technique on 3" round or square 18 ga copper, one coat of crackle on the back is adequate. My beginners' course ended with Doris Hall's paisley design, which combined many techniques, and a simple cloisonné piece on a 1" disc of fine silver.

You need to plan the sequence in order to combine techniques. Have a design and color combination in your mind or on paper, at least the beginning of it. Either start with the design and decide which technique should be used for it or decide which technique you want to use and select the metal and the base coat of enamel for that technique. You need to select either a particular mesh enamel or a liquid form enamel, a transparent or opaque and a light or dark color. All these decisions are for the base coat of enamel on the front of the metal. As you develop the piece, you need to continue to make these same decisions.

For an abstract design with areas of color, using dry or wet stencils and maybe some sgraffito areas, your choice of the base coat influences the selection of the enamel layer or layers over it in subsequent firings, e.g., a transparent blue over an opaque yellow will give you a green. With enamel, as with oil painting, you usually can cover up an unwanted fired color with an opaque enamel in the following firing, especially if you have not fired a heavy coat. If you are planning on six or more layers of enamel, then each coat, except for the base coat, should be a thin application of enamel. To add other techniques to this piece designed with stencils, transparent and opaque sifted enamels and sgraffito, a fine line black drawing could delineate all or some of the shapes you have created. There are an infinite number of choices you could make. When I first learned to enamel, I would daydream about combining an assortment of the enameling techniques.

FIRESCALE
Bare copper, when fired, develops a layer of firescale. The longer and higher the firing, the thicker the firescale becomes on the bare metal. Sometimes, especially with a thick coat, it will flake off when the piece cools after the firing. The firescale

layer expands and contracts with the firing as do metals and enamels. Most enamelists remove the firescale from the edge of a copper piece after each firing. When the piece has cooled, the firescale will usually chip off and could contaminate the enamel you are working with if you are sifting on another layer. With the firing, the color of the firescale changes after the second or third firing, from a rust tone to almost a black when a coat of flux is fired over it. (I still use this firescale line for my signature on the back of my pieces. Judy Stone describes this line in her design technique of Layering.) In addition to drawing into the base coat to expose the copper, you can cover the line with sifted flux before firing. This will produce a flux line instead of a black oxidized line. You can also combine both the flux line and the oxidized line in a design by sifting the flux over some of the sgraffito and leaving some of it bare copper.

You can also create a design with firescale. Dilute enameling gum with water 1:1. Brush the diluted gum in any shape or area on bare copper. Sift enamel over the entire piece, stand the piece on edge and tap it to remove the enamel from the ungummed areas. You then have the enamel in the design you have brushed on the piece with the diluted gum. If the enamel did not adhere everywhere you wanted it to be, you may use a small sifter to sift that same enamel over those areas. Fire at 1500°F, only to maturity. If you overfire, the firescale will be thick and could flake off if you enamel over it. The enamel areas will be edged with firescale. This technique is most effective with a pale opaque or a light color transparent for the first firing. When the piece cools, file off the firescale from the edge of the piece and brush the face of the piece to remove any loose firescale. The second layer of enamel can be flux or any light transparent enamel that is sifted over the entire piece and fired. This firing seals the firescale and your piece is ready to be developed further with additional layers of enamel.

BUBBLING THROUGH

Fire a base coat of liquid form enamel on the back and soft 80 mesh opaque enamel on the front. Fire two siftings of counter on the back. Fire high a coat of medium fusing 80 mesh transparent enamel over all or part of the piece. The soft opaque enamel will bubble up through the transparent enamel.

COMBINING A DRY STENCIL WITH THE BUBBLE THROUGH

Instead of covering the whole piece with the transparent enamel over the opaque base coat, sift transparent enamel over the edge of a plastic shield held close to the piece. The closer to the piece you hold the shield, the straighter the edge of the sifted enamel. You can also use this technique to sift one enamel color over part of another in a plaid or stripe design.

FLOWING

Fire the base coats of any enamel you like. Use a small sifter to apply areas of three or four contrasting colors, opaque and/or transparent, close to each other. Some can overlap. Spray the piece with water until a little wetter than damp and tilt the piece in various directions to guide the flow of the enamels. If the enamels do not move, you can use water in an eyedropper to make the enamel flow as you tilt the piece. When the enamel design is to your liking, hold a piece of paper towel at the edge to draw off the excess water. Sift a light coat of soft flux over the piece to absorb the remaining excess water before you fire the piece to maturity.

WET STENCILS

Fire the base coats. Cut pieces of paper towel, wet them thoroughly and place them over a fired base coat. If the paper hangs over the edge of the piece, you can remove it easily after you sift on the enamel. If there is no overhang, use a pin and tweezers to lift off the wet stencil. If the copper piece has sloping sides, you might want to spray 1:3 diluted gum over the paper after it is positioned on the piece, then sift an enamel and spray the gum again. The sifted enamel should cover only the edge of the paper stencils. The piece is dry when the gummed enamel surface feels like sandpaper. Before you fire the piece, you can sgraffito with any sharp tool into the dried enamel. If you are using only water under the sifted enamel, you can fire the piece when the enamel is just damp. The same washed stencils or new ones can be used for overlays in subsequent firings. The number of layers and firings depends on the design you envision. This is a good technique for learning how one transparent looks over a number of transparent enamels.

PULLING THROUGH

First fire the base coats in an enamel of your choice. Using the Indian sand painting method, apply about four 80 mesh enamel colors in bands of color close to each other. First try enamel colors that are in sharp contrast to your base coat. Black and white are strong colors to combine. Put the point of a sharpened chopstick just beyond an outside band and drag the point through the other colors. If you raise the chopstick a little as you get through the last color, that color will end in a point. Pull through as many times as you like.

OVERALL LUMPS

Fire a base coat of flux on the front of a shallow plate and counter enamel the back. Spray the piece with diluted 1:3 gum and sift a light coat of white or a light color opaque 80 mesh over the whole piece. Place different sizes of soft fusing lumps over the whole piece and press each lump in place, which will move aside the sifted opaque enamel under the lump. Tiny lumps can be close together because they will not spread as much. The larger lumps will expand to cover more area. When the gum is dry, the piece is fired to maturity. If you place enough lumps on the piece they will almost touch each other when they expand and spread in the firing. The opaque enamel will frame each lump. After the lumps are fired, the piece should not be fired again upside down because the lumps might droop down to the floor of the kiln.

If your lumps are too large, put a few of them in a brown paper bag that is inside a plastic bag and put the bag on a scrap of wood. Bang on the lumps with a hammer. The lumps will scatter unless they are in a bag.

DORIS HALL'S PAISLEY DESIGN

This paisley design was a commercial enamel that Doris Hall and Kalman Kubinyi produced. When I began teaching, I used this design, with her permission, as part of my beginners' course because it combined so many enameling techniques. This enamel plate is shown on page 96. The enamels were Thompson's old leaded 80 mesh and were fired around 1500°F.

Procedure

- Apply and let dry #767 Peacock crackle (now called Liquid Form Enamel) to the back of the plate.

- Sift a good covering coat of #426 soft flux on the front over diluted gum.

- Fire the piece flux side up, supported on a stilt. Front and back base coats are fired in the first firing. This method eliminates firescale forming in firing because there is no uncovered copper. All the subsequent coats are fired right side up also.

- The second firing has another coat of crackle dried on the back and transparent #200 turquoise sifted on the front with the transparent and opaque lumps gummed in place. Push aside the turquoise enamel, about the size of the ½" red transparent lumps, from eight evenly spaced areas about ½" down from the edge of the plate. This exposes the flux base coat where the red lumps are to be placed with undiluted gum. The same is done with the transparent smaller lumps in the center of the plate. Then some small opaque lumps are just pushed down into the transparent enamel. With the tip of a palette knife, a little additional #200 enamel is placed at the bottom of the large red lumps around the edge of the plate. The added enamel forms a banking shelf to support each lump in the firing. With the gum dry and all the lumps in place, fire the piece until the lumps have smoothed down.

- For the third firing, paint about a 1/8" wide line of separation enamel around each lump, leaving at least ¼" between the line and the edges of the lumps. The painted lines are connected with additional lines to form an overall design. The separation enamel, in a one ounce bottle, with an oil base has to be stirred thoroughly and a separate thin brush is kept to use just for it. The brush is cleaned with turpentine. When the separation enamel is dry, fire the piece. The painted lines, when fired, sink through to the flux and double in width.

- For the fourth firing, apply a coat of the Peacock crackle over the entire front of the piece. When the crackle is dry, sgraffito with a pointed stick or tool, following the depressed lines made by the separation enamel which exposed the flux base coat. Additional cross-hatched sgraffitto lines should be done over the lumps. The crackle will break up and the lines will widen as you fire to maturity, or a little beyond, to complete the plate.

CLOISONNÉ PENDANT ON FINE SILVER

Fine silver cloisonné wire on a flat piece of 18 or 20 ga fine silver is the simplest material to use for cloisonné. You do not have to worry about burning up the fine silver wires as you do when you fire fine silver wires on copper. I fire in a heat saturated kiln at 1500°F. The fine silver piece only needs to be cleaned in the kiln because it does not form a firescale coat as does bare copper when fired. My eperience is only with leaded enamels, so the results may not be the same with unleaded enamels.

The first cloisonné piece my students created was a one-inch 18 ga fine silver flat disc with a hole drilled for a jump ring.

Materials

- 1" 18 ga fine silver flat disk with a drilled hole for jump ring
- 1' flat, fine silver cloisonné wire, .040" x .010", for the design
- 2 oz. soft flux, washed and dried. Thompson leaded 80 mesh soft flux #426 for the front base coat or try an unleaded flux for silver
- 2 tsp. total of one or any number of 80 mesh transparent washed enamels to add color
- 1 brush full of very thin crackle for the back base coat
- 1 tsp. uncut enameling gum for adhering wires to the silver piece before firing

Tools

- Pair of pointed tweezers, with the points not very sharp, to bend the wires
- Straight blade bezel shears to cut the wires *(see photo, page 22)*
- #1 sable liner brush to wet pack the enamels
- 1" 80 mesh sifter to apply base coat of flux to front of the disc
- Carborundum stone for first stoning of top of the wires to remove any fired on enamel
- Scotch stone for final finishing of top of wires
- A wooden board to put across a sink or set-tub for stoning the wires under water

Procedure

- Trace the disc about four times on 3" x 5" index cards.

- Draw designs for the wires. For this first one keep the wires at least 1/8" away from edge.

- As you design, remember that the wires are to form cells in which the enamel will be wet packed with the brush. A wire must have a bend to be able to stand up on its thin edge. Select one design as your pattern.

- Bend and cut the wires to your pattern. It is easiest to work with a 3" length of wire. When you cut the wires, the cut must be a true straight line for the wire to butt against another wire. Each wire must also be flat against the disc. Read Joseph Trippetti's method for bending wires to the pattern. Each piece, picked up with the tweezer, is placed on the cleaned disc with uncut gum.

- When all the gummed wires of the design are in place and dry, sift the soft flux over the entire wire design area about one third the height of the wire including about an 1/8" on the outside wires of the design.

- Fire the piece on a trivet at 1500°F until the enamel is holding the wires and the enamel looks almost white. If you use the medium fusing leaded flux, #1005, it will have a yellow cast.

- For the second firing, wet pack soft flux with diluted 1:2 Klyr-Fyre around all the outside wires of the design and sloping down to the edge of the piece. Let dry and fire smooth.

- When the piece is cool, paint a very thin coat of crackle on the back. When it is dry, sgraffito your name or logo.

- Wet pack the transparent colors into the cells with the tip of the liner brush. Push the enamel grains against the wires and then fill in the cell. Multiple thin fired layers are brighter than one thick layer of enamel. Add a drop of diluted gum to each cell. In the Swiss method, the enamel is not filled to the top of the wires. You can stop filling the wires and firing when the piece is to your liking.

- At the sink, put a 3" square of chamois under the enameled disc and place both on the wooden board under the faucet in order to stone the top of the wires under running water.

- Use the coarse Carborundum stone first, stoning in a circular motion. Then the Scotch stone is rubbed along the length of the tops of the wires. The side edge of the piece is either cleaned the same way or on a polishing wheel with a Bright Boy stone. At the wheel, you rotate the edge of the piece, keeping it moving against the spinning stone.

- A sterling jump ring is set in the drilled hole, and the piece is complete.

You can also design the cloisonné piece with bent wires without drawing a design. Just bend pieces of wire and place two bent pieces on the silver in the center of the disc. The end of one piece butts against a length of the other piece. Then you add pieces to make enclosed cells, designing with the bent and cut pieces. If you are a jeweler and intend to bezel the enamel, it will be easier if your wires are 1/8" in from the edge. You can use wood dowels of various diameters to bend circles or part of a circle. A pair of tweezers and your fingers are all you need to bend the wires along with a feeling for design.

Overglaze Direct Painting
Lilyan Bachrach

For more than twenty years, I have been using overglazes as a direct painting technique. My canvas usually is a fired, flux and white base-coated enameled copper piece. Although I sometimes make a rough sketch for placement, I more often paint directly in an impressionistic style. Each painting is a new and different delight. Even after all these years, the firing process is still able to produce a surprise often enough to hold my interest when I watch the enamel change color as it cools. When the result is not acceptable or what I intended, I enjoy working my way out of a color or design error.

I make wall pieces, plates, bowls, mezuzahs, and switch plates. The switch plates and the mezuzahs are small enamels that I use to experiment with new color combinations or a new design. In my studio, my work has ranged from 1¼" cloisonné jewelry to sectional pieces comprised of 12" square segments. I use ceramic overglazes and china paints (onglaze enamels) and also mix them together to make additional colors. My overglazes are old ones, probably leaded, from Thompson Enamel and Standard Ceramic Supply Co. The china paints are from various china supply houses. Most china painters and enamelists mix the material with oils, but I use water to prepare the overglazes for painting.

In the early 1970s, I produced a series of enamels made with fine line black pen drawings and overglaze colors added with small brushes. While traveling in Canada I visited an enamel studio that had been marketing a line with the same technique. They, too, were painting flowers with the fine line black first. Shortly after that visit, I thought of using watercolor brushes first to paint the flowers and then adding the black pen line. The only overglazes I had were the limited colors that Thompson Enamel then carried. I stopped using this technique because I did not like the yellows and oranges when fired at 1500°F, and I thought the Thompson palette was inadequate. About a year later, while exhibiting at the American Craft Council Northeast Fair, I was browsing through the catalog of Standard Ceramic Supply Corp. and spotted columns of ceramic overglazes with enticing names from cream to dark purple. They fired at just under 1500°F, which was what I wanted. The sales representative told me they would not work on enamels and I would be wasting my money. I decided to try them anyway, despite his protests, and bought about 12 colors: yellows, oranges, pinks, purples and a deep blue. Most of them worked, and

I am still using the Standard Ceramic Supply product. The ones I list below are my favorites. It was not until the late 1980s that I added the china paints.

If you want to add overglazes to your supply of enamels, buy the smallest quantity of about 8-10 colors to start, or a sample kit if it is available. A teaspoon amount lasts a long time. The china paints come in a glass vial. The violets and pinks are the most expensive. I am assuming that you know how to paint in some other medium. If not, you can use them to add an accent of color or shading to an area of fired enamel on your piece made with one of the beginner's techniques.

The Standard Ceramic overglaze colors I use most are: Lemon ST114, Pink 236, Green 112-P, Canary 650/291, Dark Violet 324 and Orange 286. I use the Thompson 900 series, except the yellow and orange. Originally, I made color samples on 3" x 8" 20 ga copper that had a medium-firing white base coat and black crackle on the back. My enamels are mostly 80 mesh leaded ones from Thompson that I purchased in quantity years ago. For the base coats I usually use Thompson's leaded 80 mesh #1005 medium flux, #1000 medium white, counter enamel, #124A hard black, #772 liquid form enamel and #426 soft flux over my name on the back.

I primarily use the #169 Norman kiln on a 220V line. The inside chamber is 16" x 16" x 9". The door opens horizontally from the right side. The pyrometer is set in the right rear corner. It has two variable control switches although I would prefer one switch. It was re-bricked and rewired about 15 years ago. I have a reserve set of wires.

To prepare the overglazes for painting, I put about ½ teaspoon of each color in the bottom part of a 3" plastic petri dish near one side. The cover is labeled. I add water gradually with a syringe as I blend the overglaze to a painting consistency with a small bent painter's palette knife. My favorite knife has a ½" wide straight edge because I accidentally broke off the tip years ago. I use tap water. When I paint, I tilt the uncovered petri dish slightly so the overglaze is at the top of the dish and a little water at the bottom of the dish.

I work in a modified production style for the base coats on purchased 18 ga copper forms. If I am making 6" to 8" plates, I usually prepare about 12 pieces at a time for the paintings, which then are painted in a number of sessions. If the base coat is to be a white or light opaque, I clean the copper pieces with Penny-Brite. If the base coat is to be a transparent, I clean the copper on the polishing wheel with a goblet buff that has been charged with Lea Compound C. When clean, each piece is placed back side up on a 2" bottle to be coated with black crackle, as shown on page 45.

I brush on the crackle, let it dry and then sgraffito my name in the center with a sharpened chopstick. The loosened dry crackle is tapped off, and any dry crackle on the edge of the piece is removed with an edge of the square handle of the chopstick. The pieces are placed face side down on a tray and transferred to the enamel worktable. I heat the kiln to 1500°F and keep it there while I apply the enamel to two plate fronts. Before applying the enamel, I set up the kiln furniture to receive two pieces for firing. On each of two 6" square nichrome mesh planches I place a 3-pointed stilt for firing the piece with the front side up. While a piece fires, I apply the enamel on the next one, keeping a production line moving. This part is just work. By firing a number of pieces, one after the other, the firing hardware stays hot and prevents a big drop in the kiln temperature when the kiln door is opened.

For my usual white base coat on the front, I mix about 2 pounds of Thompson's leaded 80 mesh, #1000 white and 1 pound of their #1005 medium fusing flux in a 5 pound jar. I like the softer look with a little of the flux showing through instead of a bathtub white porcelain look. To sift enamel on a piece, I use the 60 mesh, 2" old-fashion metal tea strainers that have sloping straight sides with the mesh flat across the bottom. Some of my sifters are labeled flux, white or counter. I only use them for what they are marked so I do not have to think about cleaning them. (See section on sifting base coats.) On the front, I sift a heavy coat of the flux/white mixture and a second light coat of white. The piece is sprayed with water before and after each sifting. With a light spraying of water, just enough to hold the enamel, I do not have to wait for the piece to dry. The first piece is placed on the set-up stilt, put in the kiln and fired to maturity to ensure that the black crackle on the back is shiny and fired enough to adhere. While that piece fires, the next flux and white layers are sifted on the front of the next piece. The next piece is set on the other firing set-up, the first piece is removed from the kiln, and the next piece is put in the kiln. The program continues until all the pieces have a fired base coat on the front and on the back. This is the base coat method of firing both enameled sides in the first firing that I learned from Doris Hall in 1955.

My counter enamel, with the 60 mesh sifter, for the second coat on the back is 2/3 left over 80 mesh enamels and 1/3 Thompson's 80 mesh, leaded, 124A hard black. By having the hard black in the mixture, I do not have to re-enamel the back again. Soft flux, Thompson's #426, is sifted over my name. I sift 2 coats of counter on the back except over my name. As usual, a light spray of water is applied before and after each sifting. The same production line system is used, but with hammocks to support the plates with the back side up in the kiln. Each piece is fired to maturity. When removed from the kiln, the plate is transferred to a steel plate, back side up and weighted with an old iron until it cools. After all the pieces are fired, and loose firescale on the edges removed, the plates are ready to be painted. Each piece takes about seven firings.

I have a separate table for painting. The petri dishes, with the covers on them, are set up as a color palette. Any overglazes that have dried out have a few drops of water added and are blended smooth to prepare for painting. Two bottles containing water are also on the table, one for cleaning the brushes and the other for clean water, along with a folded paper towel for wiping a brush and the syringe and water spray bottle. I use sable or kolinsky watercolor brushes. As with any painting medium, you need to practice the brush strokes and develop your own style and preferences for colors. For painting leaves, I use Lebenzon's custom made, kolinsky, broad, long-pointed watercolor brush in the Chinese painting method. The brush is held vertically, pressing down on the heel of the brush for a broad stroke and gradually, as the brush is moved forward, pulled up off the paper for a pointed tip to the leaf. You need to remember that most china paints have lead in them and some have cadmium so do not put the brush in your mouth.

The overglazes handle like watercolor paints in that one wet color placed on another one will blend or bleed; but unlike painting on paper, the enameled surface does not absorb the overglaze. If part of the painting dries before you are ready to fire the piece, then the whole piece will need to be sprayed lightly with water. If the painting dries in sections, a line often appears between these sections when the piece is fired. The overglaze painting is dry by the time it is placed on the warm firing set-up and put in the kiln. Plates and bowls are placed in the kiln on a three-pointed stilt on the planche; plaques are fired within a hammock. I fire with my kiln at about 1500°F. It is years since I tested the pyrometer reading. I really judge the heat by the color in the kiln and fire for time by instinct and a quick peek. Overfired overglazes will lose the intensity of their colors.

For my floral painting, I often start by painting various shades of green leaves with the kolinsky watercolor brush. Next come my imaginary flowers. The first flower is often the predominating color from which the painting develops. If I do not like a part of the painting that has dried, I remove it with a small, stiff, stencil brush. If the whole composition is not to my liking, the piece is rinsed off under running water. When the painting is at the point that it cannot be developed further, it is fired to just before maturity. Then if there are areas, say on the fired green leaves, where I want to add another flower, I either sift leaded, 80 mesh, #644, soft white in a shape and size or I wet pack an opaque over a leaf. To add color to this unfired white flower, I charge a brush with color and run the tip around the outline of the shape I want. A color can also be added within the added shape. The wetter the overglaze and the enamel, the more the overglaze color will bleed into the opaque white enamel. Instead of using the stiff stencil brush to remove part of the painting, you can use a wet clean brush.

Instead of mixing a color on your palette you can blend colors on the painted section when it is wet by charging the brush with thin overglaze and letting it run either where you direct it or by tilting the piece. Most of the overglazes are transparent, but adding the white will lighten the color and also lose most of the transparency. As you work with the overglazes you learn which ones need to be applied thicker, like the reds that burn out faster than other colors.

When I consider the painting completed, I often delineate some of the shapes by drawing with Hunt's #101 nib in a pen holder (you can also use a ruling pen) and Thompson's fine line black, which I purchase in liquid form. (Some enamelists use it to sign their name on the front of their work.) I call it "ink". I order it in the 1-ounce bottle because it takes a lot of stirring to put the glob at the bottom into solution. I use a dental spatula to stir the ink well, and separate it into four little glass bottles with screw on lids. Before using the ink, it needs to be stirred well again. I first test if it flows from the nib like ink and test if I can draw some lines on smooth paper. I hold the pen almost straight up when I write with it. If the ink is too thick, add artist turpentine one drop at a time and stir after each drop. You will need to stir the solution about every ten minutes as you use it and also dip the pen in turpentine from time to time for the ink sometimes dries on the nib tip. After you dip the pen in turp you need to re-dip the nib into the fine line black a few times before you draw with it or the ink will be too thin. If you get an unwanted blob, wait until it dries and then remove it or part of it with a pointed chopstick. When the pen drawing is complete and dry, the fine line black is corrected with the chopstick. Then fire just until the drawing is smooth. You can test it, out of the kiln, with the edge of the potter's spatula. The wide areas will have break lines in them. I like that. If you overfire, the drawn line becomes thinner and, of course, the overglaze colors are changed. I finish each piece with a sifted overall veil of 80 mesh soft flux.

The final step is to smooth the exposed metal edge. My sanding and polishing wheels are connected to a dust collector purchased and installed by a local dental supply company. Even so, I don a nose mask, a facemask, leather gloves, and a shower cap over my hair before using the equipment.

The face edge of the piece is finished first at the belt sander with a 6" x 48" fine grit emery cloth belt. After grinding the front and back edge of each piece, I remove the grinding marks. I tear a sheet of fine emery cloth into 1" x 12" strips and wrap one strip around one end of a 1" wide wood stick. Wearing leather gloves, I rub with the strip of emery cloth across the grinding marks to obliterate them. As the beginning wrap of the emery cloth strip wears out, I wind it a little to have a clean area to work with. The final finish is a rubbing of the metal with a wad of 00 steel wool. I place felt tabs on the back of the piece over the three stilt marks and then add my label. Each piece is placed in a plastic bag to keep it clean.

Another use I have found for the overglazes is to make pale opaque enamel colors when I need to match a client's color swatch. For a small amount of enamel, about an ounce of 80 mesh, maybe white, is put into a 4-ounce glass jar with about 2 ounces of water and ¼ teaspoon of overglaze color in painting consistency This mixture is then well stirred and allowed to sit for about 15 minutes and stirred again. If you want it darker, gradually add more overglaze, stir and let it settle in. Pour off the excess water. Place the open jar with a loose piece of paper on top of it on top of the kiln to dry out. When the enamel is dry, you can wet pack or sift as you wish. If I am aiming for a specific match to a swatch, I often have to make a few different batches and fire samples on scrap copper.

If you like to paint, you will find the nuances of color that can be obtained with overglazes are limitless. The tactile quality of enamels as well as the sense of their enduring quality will bring you delight.

Plique-à-Jour: Russian Soldering Method
Sandelle/Sandra E. Bradshaw

There are a number of methods for plique-à-jour, a filigree technique that allows light to shine through the enamel, much like stained glass. With plique-à-jour, there is no backing for the vitreous enamel; instead a structure of metal is made with open spaces, called cells, for the enamels. I form a framework of fine silver square wire and within that framework I solder wires together in a design formed of cells. To make the framework as I do, you need to know how to use the jeweler's torch and how to solder. I use this Russian method of soldering primarily to make fine silver earrings. As the earrings dangle, the light shines through the enameled cells.

I start with rough sketches and then make an exact drawing. I keep a file of my drawings. If the earrings are asymmetrical, I also trace the drawing from the opposite direction. The cells are kept under 3/16" in width. The drawing is copied on tracing paper and trimmed with a 1/16" margin all around. The tracing paper drawing is the pattern on which I will glue the cut pieces of wire. I put this drawing on a 3" x 5" white index card and then put both on a 2" thick Styrofoam block. The drawing and card are held in place with stainless steel dressmaker straight pins, one in each corner.

I use 16 ga square, fine silver wire for the outer wire frame. The major lines of the design are 16 ga x 22 ga fine silver wire and the fill-in lines are 16 ga x 32 ga. You can use decorative wires if they are the same dimensions as the fill-in wires. I bend and cut the wires to the file card pattern with jeweler's pliers. Each wire piece, formed to match the pattern, is flattened on the steel block with a plastic hammer. The flattened segment is picked up with tweezers, dipped in Sobo white glue, and then placed on the tracing paper pattern. Be careful to keep the wires perpendicular to each other. Like the wires in cloisonné, they have to make a tight-butted joint.

When all the glued wires are in place and dry, I remove the pins and put the piece and the tracing paper on a 1/16" or 1/3" thick oxidized steel plate. The oxidization on the steel will prevent the solder from adhering to the steel plate. The plate is oxidized by being repeatedly fired in the kiln until it is black. Using 60 mm binding wire, bind the glued wires to the steel plate. First wind the binding wire horizontally

1/8" apart and then vertically also every 1/8" apart. When a piece of wire is holding every joining, the work is ready to be soldered.

The flux I use for soldering is a solution of half dry boric acid and half borax (Boraxo) mixed with warm water. About a half cup of each is put in a heat resistant glass-lidded container, like a small Pyrex casserole with a wide opening, because hot enamels will be put into it. The water is added gradually while being stirred with a thin rubber spatula until the solution is the consistency of maple syrup. It should not crystallize when it is cool. If it does, add a little more warm water and let it cool. Eventually, it will not crystallize and that is just right. The flux solution is stored in a tightly covered glass jar so it will not evaporate. A hot plate or the top of a hot kiln can warm it when you are ready to use it.

The solder is 72/28 silver/copper that comes in a bar form. Thompson Enamel and T. B. Hagstoz and Sons, Inc. sell it. I make filings of the solder bar with a clean coarse file onto a piece of clean paper. Once you start to add the solder to the piece, you have to work quickly. The wired piece is dipped into the warm flux solution and placed vertically in a bird's nest (a wad of binding wire, loosely scrunched together) to prop up the piece. I sprinkle the solder filings with my fingers into all the joints. The flux is dried with a Rosebud torch tip, using a low oxygen bushy flame. The torch burns off the tracing paper also. Then the flame is increased, and the torch is moved up evenly from the bottom to the top as the solder flows. This solder turns black when it has flowed. All joints must be touching in order for the process to work. The piece is dropped into warm boric solution to cool and then the joints are checked. If there are any loose joints, I push them together with tweezers, dip the piece in the flux solution and reapply the solder filings with a brush. It usually takes about three soldering passes to complete the soldering. When all joints survive being tugged at with the tweezers, I remove the binding wire and drop the soldered piece into fresh warm pickle of Sparex 2 solution, neutralize it in baking soda solution and rinse well. Remember to use copper tongs to remove the piece from the acid. The piece is rinsed well before the next three kiln firings.

The final step before enameling is to heat the piece in the kiln at 1430°F three times for one minute each time to bring fine silver to the surface. The first two times, the heated piece is put into water, then into an acid bath for five minutes, and then rinsed with clear water. The third time, the piece is not put in the acid bath but is either air cooled or cooled in water. Handle the piece as little as possible to avoid damaging it or contaminating it with oil from your hands.

My principle for plique-à-jour is short controlled firings that cause the enamel to just fuse to the metal cell walls. The firings must be short enough to avoid having the enamel pull from the center of the cells and run up the wires. It takes a well heat-saturated kiln to control the temperature drops when you open the kiln door. My kiln for plique-à-jour earrings is 10" x 8½" x 6" on a 110V line. To heat saturate the kiln, I fire it up to 1000°F and let it hold at that temperature for 20 to 30 minutes. Then I raise the temperature to 1450°F for firing. My kiln has a digital pyrometer, and I use a timer for firing. If you greatly overfire the piece, then you have to grind off any unwanted enamels on the wires.

I purchase 80 mesh, leaded and unleaded enamels. I wash the leaded ones with distilled water, just the amount needed for one work session. The unleaded enamels are sifted to remove the fines. The sifted enamels are separated by +150 mesh and −150 mesh. In my experience there is no difference in clarity between 150 through 80 mesh and you need all those grain sizes for your mixture of gum, water and enamel to hold in the cell. I fill the cells with the +150 mesh unleaded and the 80 mesh, washed, leaded ones. To start enameling, I make a 1:5 solution of Klyr-Fyre and distilled water and cover each enamel with it, just enough to cover each grain of enamel.

To fill the cells, I use a dental tool that has a pointed spatula on each end, one large and one small. Hold the piece in mid-air between thumb and first finger and with the tool swish a gum/enamel mixture around the inside of each cell. I rub the side of the piece with the rough edge of the tool to vibrate the excess water to the surface and even out the grains of enamel in the bubble that was pulled across the cells. The excess water is blotted away with the point of a 3" diamond shaped piece of white blotter paper.

The cells are filled from the smallest to the largest and from the inside to the outside edge of the piece. Apply a thin coat. Some cells will take just a few fillings and firings while others may take eight to ten applications and firings. It is advisable to use opaque or less transparent enamels in cells that are most likely to crack at stress points. The stress points are the areas of transition: on a bowl they are near the rim and on the shoulder; on earrings they are in any sharp corners on the shoulder of curves. You learn by experience where the stresses are on each form.

Apply enamel to all the cells before the first firing. The softer enamels will fuse first, so concentrate on those. When making a pair of earrings, put them on trivets for the firing. Set your timer at 25 seconds when you place the piece in the kiln. If any enamel becomes slightly glossy, that is your firing time. If 25 seconds is inadequate, slightly cool the piece or pieces and then time for 28 to 30 seconds. Repeat the cooling and firing a little longer until the softest enamel reaches the slightly glossy stage. Any enamels that are sugary looking will need longer time after the others have a complete film. When the softest enamels have completed cells with no holes, I move to the higher firing enamel cells that are still sugary and add five seconds to the firing time until those cells start to become glossy. The filling and firing continues until there are no holes in any of the cells and all are glossy.

I check for holes with a magnifying glass under good light. The final firing is a little longer to give a true concave transparency. That final firing could be as much as 1¼ minutes, just until the enamel starts to climb the sides and thins slightly in the center.

To finish the metal, I first remove any enamel from the wires with the airflex (332-710) wheels from Rio Grande. The metal must then be polished. To start polishing, I use the RoLoc system from Rio Grande. The diamond pads range from 180 to 800 grit for the flexible shaft. Sometimes the vibrations of the flex shaft will crack cells, so it is important to make certain the tool is well oiled to cut down on vibrations. Without a flexible shaft, you can start polishing the metal by hand with diamond papers. For my final polish I buff with tripoli and then with rouge.

Plique-à-jour is a challenging technique. This is my method now. Your job as an artist craftsman is to find creative applications for this ancient filigree technique.

Cloisonné Beads Of Fine Silver
Linda Crawford/Linda Crawford Designs

I have been making my cloisonné beads since 1996 in a variety of methods with fine silver and wires of fine silver or 24K gold for the designs. My method of fusing two domed halves of fine silver requires fewer metalsmithing skills than the other methods I use, which is why I have chosen to explain this one. Although I currently create my beads the way I describe here, the door is always open for experimentation.

I make ½", ¾" and 1" beads. The beads usually have a cloisonné design on them and require anywhere from six to 20 firings. A rule of thumb is the smaller the piece, the thinner the gauge of metal. For a one-inch bead I use 20 ga fine silver. For the cloisonné wires, I purchase 20 ga fine silver, round wire and 20 ga to 26 ga in fine gold. The wire is rolled to the size I want to use. I start by drawing the design for the cloisonné wires but I do not cut and form them until I have made the bead. I finish the bead by inserting a short piece of sterling tubing into the hole I have drilled and flanging the ends of the tubing. This protects the edges of the enamel. If I use gold cloisonné wires, then I make gold tubing. I mostly use my 9"w x 9"h x 12"d electric kiln with a pyrometer.

To support the bead or beads while applying the cloisonné wires and for the firing, I make a bead jig using an 8" square of stainless mesh. Two opposite sides are bent up 2" high, which leaves a 4" x 8" bottom. I use a wire cutter to remove every other wire from the top edge of the two bent up sides, which gives slots that will support a wire that goes through the bead. I can fire three beads at one time with this jig. For the wire going through the hole of the bead, I use a 4½" length of clothes hanger wire which I have coated with Amacote, a firescale inhibitor. My firing setup is a 6" stainless mesh (the corners have been bent down 1") with a square piece of mica on top of it to catch any dripping. The 4" x 8" support that holds the beads on the dry coated wire is placed on top of the mica.

To make the bead, I cut out two circles, drawn with a circle template, with a jeweler's saw. Alternatively, a disk cutter can be used or the circles can be ordered precut. The silver disks are annealed on a charcoal block with a propane/oxygen torch, quenched in water, dried and then domed in a dapping block with punches to begin forming the bead. I gradually move deeper in the dapping block and anneal between each depression. This process continues until I have two halves that make a sphere. On the underside of each dome, I center punch and drill a hole that will just accept the clothes hanger wire and the tubing that will line the hole. I clean up the burrs in the drilled holes with a round needle file. I make a small handle with masking tape at the top of each piece to make it easier to hold the pieces for sanding. The edges of the two halves are sanded on a steel plate with 280 grit sandpaper followed by a 400 grit sanding stick. The goal is a perfect fit. The pieces are cleaned with a water/ammonia mixture using a soft toothbrush, rinsed well and dried before fusing them together with the torch.

First I use a round burr to make a small divot in the charcoal block. The divot will support the bead. I place the bead pieces on the charcoal block and spray them with Cupronal flux which is specifically for silver. Using a soft flame, the flux on each piece is dried to a white powder with a soft flame on my Meco Midget torch with a #3 tip. Then the two pieces are placed one on top of the other to form the bead. You must be careful not to melt the bead. Heat the bead evenly, both the top and bottom. The silver will start to glow red. As the bead becomes almost shiny, concentrate the heat on the joint between the pieces. You will see the silver flow into the joint. Rotate the block so that you can fuse (flow the metal) all the way around. When the fused bead is cool, I usually texture it with a bud burr or diamond impregnated bits. Check again that the seam is completely fused. If all is good, the bead is pickled in Sparex 2 solution just long enough to clean off the soldering flux.

Next, rinse the bead and put it in a light solution of ammonia and water so that the solution goes inside the bead. Rinse the bead thoroughly under running water; making sure the inside of the bead is clean. Then burnish the bead with a glass brush to bring up the shine. While the bead is drying, cut a 4½" piece of straight coathanger wire and dip the wire in Amacote or another firescale inhibitor. When both are dry, slide the bead onto the Amacote coated wire.

The adhesive I use is CMC (sodium carboxymethylcellulose), a cellulose gum that completely burns off during the firing. CMC comes in dry form, which allows me to adjust the viscosity. You can experiment to find your favorite mixture. CMC has a limited shelf life after it is mixed with water so I only mix the amount I need for the next few weeks. I mix it by stirring the water while sprinkling in the CMC. A small enamel sifter works well for sifting the CMC into the water. CMC comes with directions, but I eyeball it for the solution.

The enamels are washed with tap water and given a final rinse with distilled water. I let the flux dry so that I can sift it on the gummed bead as a base coat. The gum is a thin coat of diluted CMC that is sprayed on. I previously used Schauer's #2A flux but since that is no longer available I use the Japanese, leaded Ninomiya N1 flux for the base coat. I apply wet enamel inside the larger beads with either a 2/0 or 4/0 rounded tip, fine sable brush, whichever size fits in the hole of the bead. This base coat is fired at 1475°F for 1½ minutes. After the piece is cool, I apply another thin coat of flux, firing for two to three minutes to maturity.

The bead now receives the cloisonné wire. I purchase dead soft, 20 ga 24K round wire and fine silver round wire that I draw down and roll to the rectangular size I want. One of the sizes I use is 29-30 ga x 17-18 ga rectangular wire made with the rolling mill set at .006. The wire is annealed during and after the drawing and rolling. The annealing can be done by placing a carefully coiled roll in the kiln.

The wires are bent to the design. Each wire also must be fitted to the curve of the bead; it is held in place with a thick CMC mixture. I use tweezers and my fingers to shape each piece. The cut and shaped piece of cloisonné wire is dipped in the CMC and placed on the bead that is on the coated wire. Only the bottoms of the cloisonné wires that touch the bead need the CMC: do not flood the piece.

There are two ways to put the wires on the bead. One way is to cover the whole bead with wire, dry it, and then fire, or put the wire on in sections. I start placing the wires at the top section of the bead. If one of the wires needs to be repositioned before it is fired, I dip the tip of my brush in distilled water and use it to move the wire. Each wire should be standing straight up on its thin edge. Let dry. Fire the bead for two to three minutes at 1475°F. An indication that the wires are adhered to the bead properly is when a thin glossy line appears at the base of each wire. Let the bead cool and adjust any wires that have not adhered properly. Be careful not to press the wires too hard because they could collapse.

The selected enamel colors are washed with distilled water and kept wet in small covered plastic or glass jars. Wet packing with just the tip of a fine, sable brush, I pick up and place the enamel in the cloisons. After one side of the bead is completed with the enamel packed to the top of the wires, the excess water is drawn off with the edge of a tissue. A tiny drop of watery CMC is applied to the damp enamel. Continue packing the enamels until the entire bead is covered with one layer of enamel. The bead is let dry and then fired for 1½ minutes at 1475°F. I underfire the first layer.

You will have to experiment with your kiln for temperature and firing time. The second firing will be for two minutes and subsequent ones built up to three minutes, which helps to ensure that the molten glass will not pool on the bead and cause an uneven surface. The layering and firing continues until the cells are filled to the top of the wires.

The enameling finished, the bead is stoned under running water. I first grind the entire surface with a 120 Alundum stone until all the wires show and the surface starts to be smooth. Then I rinse and clean the bead with a glass brush until all the small dust particles are gone. If there are any glossy depressions, those areas are re-enameled and fired for about three minutes at 1475°F. This time I stone with a 200 Alumdum stone. If there are still glossy depressions, then the filling and firing and stoning continues until they all disappear. The piece is finished by polishing it.

The bead is placed on a dop stick with wax to hold the bead easily for polishing. An enamel is always stoned or polished under or with water. I start with a 400-diamond lap wheel with a water attachment. After polishing the exposed section of the bead, I put it in the freezer for five minutes in order to remove the dop wax. The wax should just pop off the bead when you take it out of the freezer. Let the bead warm a little in your hand before placing it under running water. If there is a piece of wax that is stubborn, put the bead in the freezer again for a few minutes. When all the wax has been removed, dry the bead with a soft cloth and repeat the polishing until you have done the entire surface.

If I want to hand finish the bead, I start with 325 wet/dry sandpaper, then go to 600 and finally to 1200 grit. The bead is cleaned, under water, with a glass brush and dried before I flash fire at 1500°F for one to two minutes. The firing time depends on the size of the bead. This final firing will put a high gloss finish on the bead and will seal off any "pores" that are on the surface of the enamel. I use this finish specifically for jewelry that will be worn because I feel it protects the enamel from dirt and other contaminants.

The last step is the insertion of a piece of sterling silver tubing. I usually make my own tubing, but you can purchase tubing. Specify that it be the size you want and thin walled. The hole in the bead is made slightly larger than the tubing for the tubing to slide easily in and out of the bead. Make certain that the bead is centered on the piece of tubing. Put a scribe into an end of the tube and swing it around to flare out the end of the tube. Do the same to the other end of the tube. To complete the rivet, I use the rounded end of a small ball peen hammer. Place a tubing end on a metal plate and gently tap first in the center of the tubing and then around until the edge of the tube is curled over the bead. Complete the rivet by doing the other end of the tube.

The tube may be burnished with a burnishing tool to bring out a shine. I use a red rouge impregnated buff on the wheel to put a shine on the wires and the tube ends. After buffing with the red rouge, I soak the bead in warm water with a small amount of ammonia and dishwashing liquid and then clean it with a soft toothbrush. I draw a cotton string or a pipe cleaner soaked in the cleaning liquid through the center of the tube. When all traces of rouge are gone, I soak the bead in warm, clear water, shake off the water and let the bead dry.

The word bead comes from the Anglo-Saxon root word "bebe" that means "prayer." "Bidden" means "to pray." My fondness for beads began with the rosary prayer beads when I was a young child. My beads are not always meant to be worn, but to be used for meditation and a tool in prayer.

Enameling on Sterling Silver
P. Alexa Foley, M.A.

I enamel on various metals making a variety of pieces from post earrings to 5" x 8" framed enamels. The enameling techniques I use for sterling silver are cloisonné, champlevé and plique-à-jour. When I began enameling in 1971, it was accepted that true transparent enamels could not be used on sterling silver. After studying with Joanna Stone, I persevered with my experimentation until I developed a procedure for enameling on sterling silver. Every step is important.

My sterling enamel jewelry pieces are made with a narrow sterling frame that I cut out with a jeweler's saw blade. The same pattern is used to cut out both the bottom piece and the frame. The frame is sweat soldered to the face of the sterling piece that is to be enameled. This method eliminates the need for making a bezel setting for the enamel. I also use this method for combining champlevé with the cloisonné. Instead of making just a frame, I saw out two full size pieces and then saw out cells in which I will enamel and place cloisonné wires in either some or all of the cells.

The sterling silver needs to be accurately alloyed of no less than 92/100 silver content. Reputable refiners can do this. I specify that the sterling is to be enameled and, if possible, the sheets are to be annealed. When I use 24 ga for the enameled piece, I select 18 ga for the frame. With an enamel piece of 18 ga, I use 20 ga to 22 ga for the frame. The 18 ga base needs only one counter enamel coat. Since the thinner gauge will warp easily, it needs about three coats of counter.

I often do an exact drawing using colored pencils. From the drawing, I make templates of 20 ga to 22 ga copper as patterns for the enamel piece and the frame. I use the jeweler's saw to cut these templates; then I scribe their shapes on the sterling sheet and saw them out. If the sterling is not annealed, I coat both sides of the two pieces with soldering flux (borax and water, or Battern's) and anneal them either with a torch or in the kiln. The flux and oxide are removed in a fresh hot pickle of 1:1 nitric solution.

Caution! Remember to add acid to water. Never add water to acid. When using acid, it is advisable to wear proper gloves, long sleeves, face mask and safety goggles. Sparex may be substituted for the nitric solution. If the sterling sheet came annealed, then it only needs to soak briefly in the fresh acid solution to remove all oils. To neutralize the pickle, I add water to the solution followed by the very slow addition of small quantities of baking soda. I wash the pieces thoroughly with fresh water.

Next, I borax-flux the piece and the frame and then secure them together with binding wire to be sweat soldered with IT silver solder or tested hard silver solder if I am unable to get the IT solder. There should be no solder on the area of the metal to be enameled. I bright dip the soldered unit to remove oxides. A freshly made 1:1 nitric acid solution at room temperature is needed for the bright dip. Sparex 2 also works well. Bright dipping is the most important step in the preparation of sterling for transparent enamels. The bright dip eats away a layer of sterling silver oxide, along with a layer of sterling silver. The trick is to know when to remove the piece from the acid before irreparable damage is done by extreme acid pitting. This depletion gilding is learned with experience. The soldered piece is placed gently in the acid bath. I use a Pyrex dish with a cover for the acid. Bubbles that rise to the surface of the metal are removed periodically by brushing across the piece with a long feather. When the piece is very dark, uniform gray in most places (it will be darkest around the solder seam), it is removed from the bright dip bath with wooden or plastic tongs, rinsed, neutralized with baking soda, rinsed and cleaned with a glass brush.

I put on rubber gloves to protect my skin from the minute glass threads that break off and can stick tenaciously and painfully. I rub the metal lightly with a glass brush in a circular motion under running water to minimize breakage of the glass brush. The glass brush removes the black residue of oxide that the acid brought to the surface.

At this point, the piece may be domed evenly and slightly with a rawhide mallet by striking the face of the piece that is held over a steel stake. The findings are soldered on the back with as little IT solder as possible, the firescale removed again and the piece glass-brushed as before. The piece is now ready to be enameled.

I use 80 mesh, transparent, unleaded enamels. I also purchase these enamels in lump form that I grind with a mortar and pestle when I am ready to use them. I prefer grinding my own. I wash the enamels, about a tablespoon of each ground color, with distilled water until the water is clear. To make the enamels absolutely clean, a few drops of nitric acid are added to a pint of water and the enamels are then re-washed in this solution. A final washing with clean water is required to rinse away the acid water. I have found that unused wet enamel powder tends to break down and become discolored if stored.

The first coat of enamel is hard fusing to prevent that coat from bubbling through subsequent coats of medium and soft fusing enamel. I wet pack damp enamels with thin to medium size horsehair brushes. I also use a curved dental tool, the double-ended stainless steel kind that has one end shaped like a little scoop. The frame, of course, is not enameled. I wet pack the back first, add a few drops of uncut Klyr-Fyre on the enamel and then draw off any of the excess water with a piece of tissue. When the enamel has partially dried or become tacky, the piece is turned over to enamel the front side. There I wet pack Thompson's silver flux #757, especially if I plan to use transparent reds or pinks; otherwise, I sometimes wet pack the transparents as the base coat. Though leaded enamels yield better colors in the reds, I feel safer staying with the unleaded enamels. The piece is placed on a trivet to dry and then fired just to maturity in my 110V electric kiln at about 1350°F. I use a pyrometer, but my sixth sense tells me when to peep in the kiln.

Next comes placing of the cloisonné wires with uncut Klyr-Fyre. For gold wire, I hammer 22K, 16 ga or 18 ga round wire into the rectangular thinness I want. The wet packing, drying and firing is repeated three to five times until the fired enamel is slightly higher than the frame rim.

Finishing is done by stoning under water, first with a coarse Carborundum stick and then a medium-grain one. The grinding continues until all enamel is removed from the frame and the wires, leaving the enamel even. The dull enamel surface is thoroughly washed and glass-brushed to remove any grains of Carborundum. For a final finish there is a choice. The surface of the enamel may be rubbed with fine paste-wax polish on the fingertips for a matte finish, or the piece may be flash-fired in the kiln for a glossy surface.

If the piece is flash fired, the exposed sterling silver frame will need to have the oxidation removed. This removal is a delicate matter because the enamel should not be scratched. I use tripoli or white diamond compound on a hard felt buff on a regular polishing motor. I strongly suggest that if you have not used a polishing motor that you either take a jewelry class or have someone knowledgeable show you how to use the equipment. You can be hurt badly if you are inexperienced or careless. Care must be taken not to overheat the piece with the polishing wheel or else the enamel will crack. If you remove the piece from the wheel when your fingers become hot, you will be safe. When the oxide has been buffed off, a soft flannel buff charged with rouge is used for a final polish of the sterling silver frame. If the piece is a pin, the pin stem is attached to the findings that were soldered on before enameling. For small surfaces and getting into crevices with buffing wheels, I use the Dremel electric tool following the same progression of buffing wheels with white diamond, tripoli and red rouge.

For plique-à-jour earrings, I bend and hard solder sterling silver 14 ga round wire in the shape of a fish or a bird and then flatten the forms with hammers. Sometimes I solder on a jump ring before the depletion gilding. Sometimes I drill a hole for the earwire. The sterling is prepared for enameling as previously described. After hot pickling and rinsing the frame, it is placed on a sheet of mica and then on the firing planche. The enamel will not adhere to the mica. The enamel is wet packed with transparent enamels, dried and fired. This process is repeated until the fired enamel is at the edge of the rim of the frame. The piece is stoned gently under running water until no enamel is on the frame. The piece is flash fired, and the sterling silver frame is polished after the mica sheet is removed.

I have always had a small fire extinguisher in my studio, but, fortunately, I have never had to use it. One needs to respect and approach with caution acids, electrical equipment and other tools to be able to work safely.

Gold Alloys:
Champlevé and Bàsse-Taille
Edward J. Friedman

Champlevé and bàsse-taille are two enameling techniques that are often used together. In bàsse-taille, the metal has a design that can be made in various ways. The textured metal is covered with transparents to allow the design to be seen. I make a design in the metal with gravers or texturing punches. The champlevé technique has lower areas, cells, to be filled with enamels. The champlevé technique ordinarily uses opaque enamel in the cell. However, if the bottom of these cells is textured, it is enameled with transparents. I use both of these enameling techniques in the manufacturing of rings, pendants, jewels, wedding rings and bands. My work is done on 10K, 14K and 18K in both yellow and white gold as well as platinum.

I purchase standard sheet and casting grains containing about 2% zinc. In trade work, many clients send cast pieces to be enameled. When I do not know the alloy of the metal, it is very important to clean the metal and depletion gild it after the soldering and before enameling. I either fabricate or cast my piece to be enameled and then anneal it to soften it for engraving. Next I lay out the cells, which should not be more than .6 mm deep. If the cells are deeper, the enamel will crack due to the different rates of cooling between the metal and the enamel. Many pieces are die struck to create the cell areas.

For hand engraving the outline of a cell, I use a sharp onglette graver about 3/10 mm deep. Next, using a flat graver the same size as the width of the gap between the onglette cuts, I lower the base of the cell to the desired depth. It is important to keep sharp crisp corners and a flat bottom in the cell. To texture the bottom of the cell, I use either the same flat graver to do a wiggle cut or I use a florentine graver.

It is important that all soldering is completed before enameling. Some pieces, such as catches for pin backs, bails or jump rings need to be soldered with the highest melting temperature solder for that alloy. Many of my pieces have at least five separate enameled sections that will need to be assembled to complete the finished jewel. These enameled pieces need to be tube set from the back. The tubes must be soldered in place prior to enameling. After all soldering is completed, all pieces must be depletion gilded, which removes any copper from the surface of the metal and leaves a layer of fine gold.

To depletion guild, you must anneal the metal without a fire coat by first coating the piece with boric acid and alcohol solution, torching the piece, letting it cool until all red color leaves the metal, and then quenching the piece in water. The piece is pickled in Sparex 2 for several minutes until all oxides are removed and then it is rinsed in water. I use a fine brass brush to clean the piece before placing it into a cool nitric acid bath for no more than one minute. It is rinsed and placed in the ultrasonic for further cleaning. The entire depletion process is repeated three to four times to remove all copper from the surface of the metal. The process is complete when the surface has an appearance of a muddy high karat film over the entire piece. If copper is left on the surface, it can come into contact with the enamel and change its color. White, red and green are the most susceptible to this effect in both opaque and transparent enamels.

I purchase leaded enamels in 80 mesh. The transparents in leaded enamels have a deeper color and tend not to crack as often as unleaded enamels. Powdered enamels should be kept in airtight opaque containers to protect them from air and light. I prepare only the amount of enamel needed for the day's work. First I grind the enamel with a mortar and pestle to a fine grainy consistency. Then I wash it with distilled water until the water is clear. This result takes about eight washings. The washed enamel is placed in a small container and is wetted with distilled water when it is used.

To wet-lay the enamel, I use a scoop that I made from an old file. I hammered one end into a spoon shape about 1 mm in diameter. I do not use gums, but lick the object because the saliva acts as an adhesive. I do not counter enamel the champlevé pieces because the layer of enamel in the cells is relatively thin.

The first layer of enamel fills the cell to excess to ensure a full fill and to protect the surface of the metal. As the enamel flows over the surface, it covers the entire area around the cell. The enamel keeps the oxides from forming in the metal area in and around the cell. Using the scoop, I tap the edge of the piece to pack the enamel grains tightly together. The piece is set aside to air dry before firing.

About half of my enameling is with the torch, and the other half is kiln enameled. I use an oxygen/propane mix with a Meco torch with a #4 tip for most of my torch enameling. I hold the piece in the air with an insulated spring tweezers while heating from the under side to bring the enamel to its flowing point. I have 2 kilns: one is 3" x 3" x 4" and the other is 4½" x 4½" x 6" with a pyrometer. I fire at 1500°F to fuse the enamel to the metal quickly. So not to melt the metal, I set a timer to one minute, which gives me about five seconds before a complete flow of the enamel occurs. I fire all firings to maturity.

After each firing, the piece is placed on a warm charcoal block with a watchmaker's tin on top to cool. For a larger piece, I use an Altoids (small candy) tin with the lid removed. This step ensures that the piece cools slowly and so minimizes the chance of the enamel cracking. During the cooling process, some of the enamel may chip off and need to be refilled. Refilling will have to be done two to five times to bring the enamel flush with the surface of the metal. Between each repacking, the enamel is ground down smooth and level with the surface of the metal, and the piece is placed in the ultrasonic cleaner and the steamer. This cleaning process removes any particles of ground enamel and any parts of the grinding stone from the crevices and cracks that could contaminate the next firing. I use a diamond hone of medium grade.

When the cell is fully enameled, the piece is placed in a Sparex 2 pickle solution for no more than a couple of minutes to remove the oxides. If you leave the piece in the pickle too long, the acid will etch the enamel and, in turn, the enamel will have to be removed. Removing the enamel means that the whole process will have to start again from the beginning. Next comes sanding the metal and enamel with a 400 Corundum and a 4/0 emery sandpaper. The sanding gives the surface of the metal a semi-polished finish and makes the final polishing easier. The process of stoning scratches the metal, so the metal must be smoothed before the final firing.

After the pickle, I rinse the piece and finish cleaning with a glass brush, which will not scratch the surface of the enamel. Prior to any enameling between firings, always use the ultrasonic and steamer to remove all particles in the cell and on the enamels, ensuring a clean surface prior to the next fusing. If you do not have a commercial steamer, you can use a cappuccino maker for steam.

The enameled surface should be smooth after sanding with the 4/0 emery paper. Occasionally the surface of the enamel may be rough and uneven. If so, I use a 6" round, 1" wide lap or hard felt wheel with a catch tray underneath. The catch tray is filled with pumice flower powder mixed with water, forming a paste that should have no lumps. The lap is charged to polish the surface of the metal and the enamel.

After the numerous firings, the metal will have a thick oxide scale that must be removed. Pickling does not remove this scale. To remove it, I use bobbing compound on a ¾" boar bristle brush in my flexshaft. To finish the outside of the piece, I use a 6" yellow muslin buff on my polishing lathe. Rinse and finish the piece with red rouge, polishing to a final luster.

Gold Cloisonné Wire On Fine Silver
Falcher Fusager
Magick/Fusager-Demski Design

Susan Demski and I have developed a cloisonné technique for our jewelry, which ranges in size from ¼" dia. to about 4" x 5". Our pieces are enameled on fine silver with gold cloisonné wire and then set in karat gold. For the enameling, we use 22 ga for earrings and 20 ga for most other pieces. We prefer the fine silver because it is a bright, neutral color that does not oxidize. Our enamels require from 15 to 20 firings.

We start with an exact color drawing. We either cut the shape from the drawing with table shears or order the pieces precut to our specification. The fine silver piece is cleaned with sandpaper and then slightly domed.

Next the front is usually engraved, as in bàsse-taille, in continuous lines for reflection or in intricate designs as a decorative element. We use a Dremel electric engraver. Sometimes the design is stamped or rolled in the metal.

The enamels we use are 80 mesh, leaded, in both transparents and opaques. The enamels are washed with a final rinse of distilled water. The counter enamel is purchased already mixed. It is sifted dry on the back, about ½ to 1 mm thick. Firings are at 1450°F. The base coat on the front is usually medium or hard flux that is sifted on dry and fired to maturity. If this sifted fired layer does not completely cover the metal, another application of flux is fired. Then come the gold cloisonné wires.

We purchase fine gold wire in various gauges, from 28 ga to 14 ga, which are rolled to different thicknesses starting at 2/1000". We use various size wires in each piece. The thin wire is used for small details. We bend and cut the wires to the design with fine tweezers and tiny scissors. The wires are placed on the fired flux coat with uncut Klyr-Fyre. When the gum is dry, the piece is fired until the wires are embedded in the flux.

We have three kilns, all about 12" x 12" x 7" with a pyrometer and a rheostat set at 1450°F. We fire from one to twenty pieces at a time. Each piece is placed on a high-fire steel trivet, and the trivets are placed on a steel rack. The rack is supported by two spaced bricks on the floor of the kiln.

The colored enamels are wet packed with distilled water and applied in a thin layer with a small scoop and a needle under magnification. Special care must be taken to pack the grains tightly because enamel liquefies on the surface first, trapping any air left between the grains during build-up. Besides creating problems during the final polishing, trapped air bubbles lower the brilliance of the enamel. The key to success is thin layers and tight packing.

Pieces can be tightly packed by lightly tapping the side of the piece with a tool, but we use the vibrating edge of an electric engraver held to the side of the disk. After vibrating the piece, we soak up any excess water with a piece of paper towel. The enamel piece is dried on the top of the kiln and then fired. This process is repeated for each layer. The number of layers possible depends on how thinly each layer is applied and the height of the cloisonné wire.

The layering of the enamels enables shading, which can greatly accentuate the color and give a great feeling of depth. We shade by packing grains of various shades of the same color next to each other. In this fashion, you can start with clear enamel on one end and finish with very dark enamel on the other end to create a high dynamic range. In subsequent layers, the different hues are shifted slightly to overlap the colors below. This usually requires from five to ten layers. When the enamel reaches the top of the wires, the piece is ready for finishing.

The final finishing of the enamel is done first with an aluminum oxide #80-100 belt on an expandable rubber drum and polished with a #600 belt. The drum is 8" diameter and 3" wide. It is the regular stone cutting type set up with water. At this point, there is a choice. If there are no air bubbles in the enamel, the enamel can be polished with cerium oxide for a wonderfully smooth surface or it can be flash fired at 1500°F just until the surface is glossy. We prefer a flash firing because it is a more durable surface and enhances the brilliance of the enamel.

And that's it. Your gem, the precious enamel, is now ready for its gold setting.

STENCILS AND WATERCOLORS
JENNY GORE

One of my favorite techniques for achieving almost any kind of imagery is sifting dry enamels with cut or torn stencils. Over almost 30 years of enameling, I have developed several different methods for specific purposes and combining many techniques in one enamel piece. It is part of the challenge.

When working on commissions, and as I did in my early work, I begin the process by designing on paper and preparing a working drawing. Unless the enamel is to be a very large one, the drawing is true to size. This drawing is used as the pattern for cutting the stencils. For the stencils, I use acetate or drafting film, which will not disintegrate or stretch out of shape when it is wet. Areas of the drawing are colored with pencils to make the process easier, using one color and one layer of film for each layer of enamel. I then use the same color of waterproof marking pen to trace the areas to be cut. If necessary, some registration marks are made, keeping in mind the order of firing, e.g., the higher firing colors first and the softer ones near the final coats of enamel. Sometimes more than one color can be used in the same layer if the shapes do not touch each other.

On the drawing I number each piece, both the positive and the negative, and transfer the same numbers to the corresponding layer of film. For a complicated design, all the stencils marked in the same color should be kept in separate containers as they will be used several times, depending on the number of firings.

For some applications I prepare a collage using cut or torn paper from magazines. I arrange them on a paper of the same color as my base coat, and when satisfied with my design, paste them into position. If these are to be used to show a client, I mount them on board and cover with transparent shiny film. I usually make a test piece in enamel also as the papers are seldom in colors found in enamel. This is a good opportunity to experiment with color mixing, especially with opaques, taking care to test them together before using them on the piece.

In recent work, I have allowed the design to "happen." I cut or tear stencils and build up layers of colors and shapes intuitively. This method is very much more fun than carefully planning everything and often leads to quite unexpected imagery. My individual enamel pieces range from 2" square up to 16" square. However, I can build up units of these to any size. I have several kilns. The largest is 17" x 17" x 12". The one I use the most is the 11" x 11" x 4". The small one, 6" x 6" x 4", I use only for test pieces. Here in Australia we have 240 volts.

I use 1 mm (about 18 ga) copper as a base for my wall pieces and 1.2 mm (about 17 ga) thickness for the larger pieces. The copper is cleaned with Amway metal cleaner and rinsed before sifting 80 mesh counter enamel on the back. The piece is fired. Unless I want to use the firescale as a part of the design, it is removed with diluted nitric acid, followed by a detergent wash.

For the front, I sift on two coats of medium fusing white and fire the piece. I stone the edges with Carborundum stone to remove the scale and any enamel from the edges and clean with detergent between all firings. Then the first layer of color can be applied. I like working on a base coat of either white or black. I use the medium fusing for the base coat for I find that a harder enamel sometimes causes craze or stress lines in the top coats.

To use the stencil, I spray the piece lightly with diluted Klyr-Fyre, position the first stencil and press it flat. I then spray a mist of the diluted gum over the stencil also; using a spray gun and an air compressor, although aerosol spray packs or pump action spray bottles will achieve the same result. As I sift enamel over an area, I spray it lightly to hold the enamel in place, especially if the area is to be sgraffitoed. The piece is placed on top of the kiln to dry. The kiln temperature ranges from 800°C (1470°F) to 850°C (1560°F) degrees for the early layers and drops back to 750°C (1380°F) to 800°C (1470°F) near the end, for two to three minutes depending on the size of the enamel piece.

Each further layer of color and shape follows, with any drawing by sgraffito or textural effects included along the way. If it is necessary to reuse a stencil, it can be scraped clean of enamel and rinsed to avoid contaminating colors.

When all layers are completed, some areas of fine silver or 24K gold foil may be fused to the surface and covered with well-washed transparent enamels by dry sifting or wet inlay. Any writing or drawing may be done with a pen using ceramic oxides or Carefree Luster. Sometimes these pieces have as many as thirty firings and along the way they tend to "grow," which means that stencils often have to be re-cut to fit precisely. With this technique, extremely complicated imagery with precise edges and fine detail is possible.

WATERCOLOR TECHNIQUE

The copper base is prepared as for stencils, but the ground coats of enamel on the front are preferably white or a light opaque color in a medium fusing enamel. This fusing quality is necessary because most painting enamels are very finely ground and fire at a lower temperature: they are susceptible, therefore, to burning out easily if overfired. I apply and fire at least two thin coats for the front base. If I want a textured or watercolor paper effect, I leave the second coat at the orange peel stage, slightly underfired.

Thompson's pans of watercolors supplied in a waxy base are used either alone or in conjunction with other painting or screening enamel powder. I mix the watercolors with water and do not mind if they do not totally dissolve, as this gives a grainy look on the textured background. I first mix enough water in each pan of color to make either the painting or pouring consistency needed. You only need small quantities, and the pans last for ages. I use them on very small pieces (100 x 100 mm square — about 4" square). If I am using the fine powdered painting enamels, I stir them first with water, and then mix them on a piece of glass or on a plate with a palette knife.

When the application is completely dry, it may be worked on with sgraffito tools and any undesirable areas removed. After firing at about 750°C (1380°F) for about two minutes, other layers may be added as desired. Transparent or opaque colors may be sifted on to complete the imagery in addition to accents of foils, leaf, writing or drawing with ceramic oxide or Carefree Lusters.

As you have probably deduced, my method of working comes from many years of firing enamels and mostly knowing what will happen in the firing process. It is the little surprises that make this an intriguing medium.

Overglaze Direct Painting
Lilyan Bachrach

Lilyan Bachrach fell in love with enameling after taking a course in 1955 with Doris Hall. At the Worcester Center for Crafts she studied silversmithing, jewelry, pottery, woodworking, photography, color and design. In the early 1960s, she studied cloisonné with Joseph Trippetti. She graduated from the Worcester Art Museum School, Fine Arts major in 1968. In addition to enameling commissions, she has sold her Bachrach Art Enamels since the 1970s and at the ACC Northeast Craft Fairs to galleries and shops across the country. *See page 59*

8" flower plate, 18 ga copper, enamel, fine line black, overglazes.
Photo by John I. Russell

Plique-à-Jour: Russian Soldering Method
Sandelle/Sandra E. Bradshaw

Sandra Bradshaw has been producing enamels since 1974. At age 18 she loved figure drawing; at 21 she discovered enameling and has continued the study of both since then in college and in private classes. In addition to plique-à-jour jewelry, she also creates small sculptures and watercolor paintings. Her teachers in plique-à-jour were her former business partner, John Ryan, and his original teacher, Valeri Timofeev.

See page 65

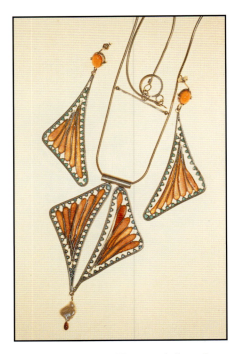

Pendant: 3" x 2" x .2" enamel, fine silver

Cloisonné Beads Of Fine Silver
LINDA CRAWFORD/LINDA CRAWFORD DESIGNS

Linda Crawford was born in Corona, CA. She has studied oil painting, drawing, jewelry fabrication, ceramics, weaving, art history and cloisonné enameling. In 1995, she turned to cloisonné enameling full time. She teaches workshops on cloisonné enameling at the California Institute of Jewelry Training in Sacramento. Her cloisonné jewelry is shown and sold throughout the United States. With two other jewelers she maintains a working studio gallery, Mendocino Jewelry Gallery, Mendocino, CA. Her themes blend the energies of spirit and nature.

See page 69

Center bead, ¾" dia, enamel, cloisonné on fine silver. Chain is hand woven fine silver. All metal hand fabricated.   Hap Sakwa Photography

Enameling on Sterling Silver
P. Alexa Foley, M.A.

P. Alexa Foley began enameling in 1971. She studied with Joanna Stone, and then persevered with experimenting until she developed her method for enameling on sterling. She spent many years as a successful enamelist, creating cloisonné, champlevé and plique-à-jour enamels. As a realtor with a GRI, she now resides in Maui, HI where she does some enameling and painting. In June 2001, Alexa received her M.A. in Cultural Anthropology and Transformative Learning.

See page 75

Tree of Life: Meditation necklace, 3" x 6" champlevé, sterling, fine silver, opaque enamel.

Gold Alloy Enameling
Edward J. Friedman

Edward Friedman, master platinum smith, has been designing and fabricating jewelry for over 25 years. He taught for Rio Grande and Precious Metals West. He is a Senior Instructor of jewelry arts at The Revere Academy of Jewelry Arts, San Francisco, CA, where he also teaches enameling. He owns The Buehn Company, a Masonic manufacturing company, which introduced him to enameling in 1997. He is also master model maker and manager, Casting Division, Hoover & Strong, Richmond, VA.

See page 79

Past Commander Pin: three-section pin, 4¾" x 1½", 4K, 10K, enamel, champlevé, engraved, die struck, cast, fabricated.

Gold Cloisonné Wire On Fine Silver
FALCHER FUSAGER of MAGICK/FUSAGER-DEMSKI DESIGN

Falcher Fusager, born in Denmark, moved to the United States in 1973. While working as a street artist, he gradually transformed his art to enamel cloisonné jewelry. He is self-taught in all areas of his work.

Susan Demski, born in Chicago, IL, moved to California in 1972. She received a BA in Art, emphasis in enameling, from San Diego State University in 1976. She was a commercial interior designer until 1985 when she focused on enameling. They formed their company, Magick, in 1988. *See page 83*

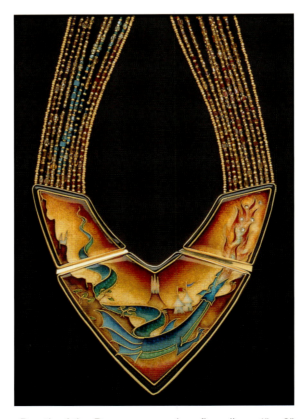

Breath of the Dragon: enamel on fine silver, 4" x 3", 24K gold cloisonné wire, 18K gold setting with diamonds. Antique beads by Martin Kilmer.

Stencils and Watercolors
Jenny Gore

Jenny Gore, of Adelaide, South Australia, was trained in graphic design and is a self-taught enameller. She started enameling in 1973. She works mainly on wall pieces and some jewelry. She has exhibited and/or given workshops in Europe, England, the United States, India, Japan, Mexico, Korea and Australia.
See page 85

The River is Wide . . . The Path is Near: 13½" x 13½" enamel on copper, 24k gold and fine silver foils, 24k gold leaf fused to surface.   Trevor Fox Photography

Paisley Design
Doris Hall

Doris Hall Kubinyi (1907-2001) was an artist and an innovator in the field of enameling. She and her late husband, Kalman Kubinyi, graduated from the Cleveland Institute of Art in 1929. In the 1940s they concentrated on enameling. They had a gallery and studio in Gloucester, Massachusetts, then downtown Boston, and a final studio move to Stockbridge, Massachusetts. They received many awards and commissions, the largest being the enamel globe at the Babson Institute. Doris and Kalman are remembered as warm and gracious friends.

See page 54

Top plate: 4", 18 ga copper, opalescent crackle over soft flux, transparent lumps in center, turquoise transparent border. Bottom plate: 6", 18 ga paisley design.
Photo by J.A. Perry

Foils: Fine Silver and 24k Gold
Marianne Hunter

Marianne Hunter had been a painter and crafts explorer when she began enameling in 1967. She is self-taught. After 12 years of discipline in the grisaille technique, she turned to color and foils that gave her a feeling of limitlessness. Her metalsmithing techniques are her own, the necessity of concept driving the ability to execute. Everything about her work is personal; it is driven by passionate yearning. Enamel work has been her only employment since 1967. *See page 121*

Kabuki Kachina Mondrian Midnight: copper base, 24K and .999 silver foils, enamel is 2½" x 2½", opals, princess cut diamond, abalone pearl, beads are tanzanite, 22K gold and apatite. Setting: 24K, 14K, and sterling silver fabricated, embossed and engraved.

Photo by G. Post

Decals and Ceramic Pencils
June E. Jasen

June Jasen began enameling full time in 1979. She has participated in numerous national and international exhibitions, competitions and received many awards. June has given workshops and lectures in the United States and in Europe. Her work is included in several archives, corporate, and private collections.

See page 123

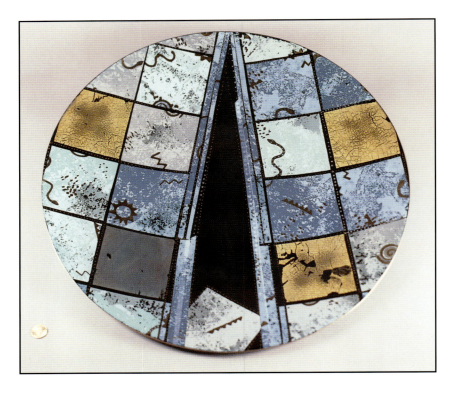

Shallow Bowl: 18" diameter, enamel on copper, decals, gold and palladium leaf, and lusters.

Large Mosaic Enamels
Jean Foster Jenkins

Jean Jenkins was professor of jewelry, design and enameling at El Camino College, Torrance, CA. She received a BFA in Art and Education, 1943 Carnegie-Mellon; MA in Art, UCLA 1967; Cranbrook 1975. Her first enameling instructor was Kenneth Bates, Cleveland Art Institute. Jean's focus has been on mosaic enamel wall pieces ranging up to 5' x 7'. Her enamel work has been shown nationally and internationally. Her studio is in Palo Alto, CA. *See page 127*

Allegory-Silicon Valley: 5' x 7' copper, foils, enamel.

Enamel Crayons
John Killmaster

John Killmaster, (b. 1934) Professor Emeritus of Art, has taught at Boise State University since he moved to Idaho in 1970, after receiving his MFA from Cranbrook Academy of Art. Currently he is listed in *Who's Who in American Art* and *Who's Who in the West*. Exhibitions of his work include: Denver Art Museum, San Francisco Museum of Modern Art, Smithsonian, American Watercolor Society in New York, and throughout the world.

See page 131

Guanajuato Couple: 11½" x 9" steel, crayons, airbrushed and painted enamel watercolors.

Champlevé With Ferric Chloride
Audrey Komrad

After graduating from New York University, Audrey Komrad started her artistic career as an oil painter, for which she received international recognition. Since 1970 she has concentrated on champlevé and cloisonné in enameling. She has taught extensively. Her list of awards and exhibitions is lengthy. Her work is in several books. She was a founder of Enamel Guild South and presently serves on the executive board of The Enamelist Society. *See page 135*

Pendant: 2½" champlevé enamel.

Portrait With Enamel Watercolors
Ora K. Kuller

In her last year at Art College for teachers in Israel, Ora Kuller was introduced to enameling. In the United States she studied enameling with Judy Danner and jewelry with Becky Brannon. In a workshop with Rebecca Laskin, she learned special enameling techniques. These teachers changed her life as an enamel artist. The magic and beauty of enameling captured her. She gives enameling workshops and works in her Belmont, MA studio, developing her own way of portraying her thoughts and dreams through enameling. *See page 141*

"Tamar" Plaque: 9" x 11", segments are 5" x 3" and smaller. 18 ga copper, fine silver foil, fine silver cloisonné wires, enamel watercolors.

Torch Firing
Deborah Lozier

Deborah Lozier is a full-time metalsmith in Oakland, CA. She received her BFA from Arizona State University, Tempe in 1984. She has focused on developing enamel and patina torch firing on copper forms. She teaches and exhibits internationally. Her work is in the permanent collection of the Oakland Museum of California. Publications include *Ornament*, *Metalsmith*, *American Craft* and the book, *Color on Metal*. *See page 145*

Wedding Crown: 4" x 3" x 3" torch fired enamel, copper.

Vessel Forms
Sarah Perkins

Sarah Perkins received her BA in Art from San Diego State University in 1979 and an MFA from Southern Illinois University in 1992. She is Associate Professor of Art and Head of the Metals program at Southwest Missouri State University and a Trustee of The Enamelist Society. Her work has been shown extensively in the United States and abroad and also has been published in *Ornament*, *American Craft* and *Metalsmith* publications. *See page 151*

Blue Intersections: 8¼" x 5" copper, silver, enamel.

Cloisonné Jewelry With 24k Wires
MERRY-LEE RAE

Merry-Lee Rae has been making jewelry since 1966 when she joined her father in the garage while he dabbled in metal arts. In 1976 she fell in love with enameling, and her life took a turn from hard-core academics to a relentless, obsessive pursuit of crafts. She feels privileged to have the support of her extraordinary family. She sees herself as a dedicated romantic. Her awards and achievements, the shows, the galleries, the private collections, and the lack of training are not as important to her as the people who are touched by her work.

See page 155

Mermaid Treasure: 1½" wide, 26 ga domed fine silver, 24k gold wire, river pearl, fabricated 18k gold setting.

ELECTROFORMED VESSELS
JUNE SCHWARCZ

June Schwarcz (b.1918) in Denver, CO. She is a Fellow of the American Craft Council and received their Gold Medal. The museum collections that have her work include Metropolitan Museum, Renwick Gallery of the Smithsonian, and Kunstgewerbe Museum in Zurich, Switzerland. Mostly she makes electroformed, three-dimensional objects. The richness and brilliance of transparent enamels still fascinates her after 47 years of enameling. *See page 159*

#2114 Vessel: 10" x 5¾" x 3½" x 3½"
electroformed copper, enamel.

Large Cloisonné On Copper
Marian Slepian

Marian Slepian's site-specific installations for public spaces are seen nationally, and collectors have been accumulating her work for 35 years. Recently she has been making objects in fine silver, particularly for ritual use. She graduated from the Fashion Institute of Technology. Studying with Joseph Trippetti formed the basis for her enameling career, although she was self-taught prior to that. She currently teaches enameling at the Newark Art Museum. *See page 163*

Concerto D'Arourjuez: 13" x 27" copper, fine silver wire, enamel.

Layering Over Sgraffitoed Liquid Enamel Base Coat

JUDY STONE

Judy Stone lives in the San Francisco Bay Area and has been enameling professionally since 1972. She supports herself from the sale of her work. Her life revolves around enameling. She teaches it. She advocates for it. She probably dreams about it, although she never can remember her dreams. The imagery in her work, while mostly abstract, has reference to floating forms lurking in her subconscious. She has developed her own way of working based on availability of enameling supplies and the contemporary work of the late Fred Ball.

See page 167

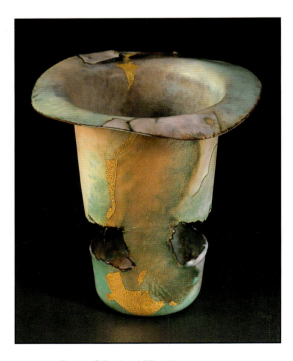

Burnt Offering VIII: 18 ga copper, spun vessel form, plasma cut, riveted, gold foil, satin finish, enamel.

GRISAILLE AND LIMOGES
MONA SZABADOS

Mona Szabados was born in Oslo, Norway. She has been enameling since 1980 and is mostly self-taught. Her goldsmith husband, Alex Szabados, makes all of the gold and stone settings for her enamels. *See page 171*

Locket: 1½"w x 2½"h x ¾"d copper, enamel,
Foils: 24K, fine silver, and palladium.
Stones: opal, diamond, sapphire.
Setting: 22K bezel, 18K gold.

Risso Screen
Joann Tanzer

Dr. Tanzer, Professor Emeritus of Art, taught at San Diego University for 36 years. In 1960 she developed their enameling degree program. The permanent collections that have her enamels include the Decorative Art Museum, Moscow, Russia; Limoges Museum of Enamels, Limoges, France; Hiroshima City, Japan and many private collections. Her exhibits include Tokyo, Japan; Limoges, France; Colberg, Germany; Barcelona, Spain, as well as many national juried and invitational exhibitions. *See page 173*

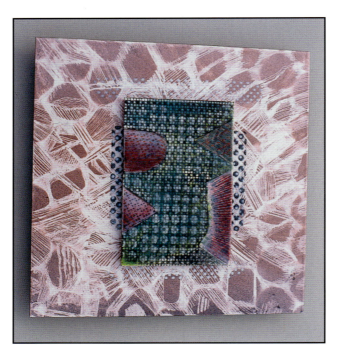

A Code Of Its Own: 10" x 10" steel,
silk screen, sgraffito, enamel.

Cloisonné On Steel
JOSEPH TRIPPETTI

When Joseph Trippetti returned from the Army in 1946, he studied for three years at Philadelphia College of Art and the fourth year at Sheffield College of Arts and Crafts in England, where he majored in silversmithing. He has been enameling since the 1950s. For some years he taught enameling and painting before concentrating on commissions and gallery exhibitions. The medieval tapestries still influence his designs. His cloisonnés were on domed copper plaques before he turned to large steel tiles. *See page 177*

Musician: 16" x 16", silver cloisonné wires, steel, enamel.

Precious Metal Clay-Silver Enameling
Jean Vormelker

Synthesizing an eclectic educational background, Jean Vormelker brings a unique perspective to her jewelry and enameling work. She has studied in the United States, Japan, Australia and Canada, and is responsible for her own development. A multi-faceted person, skilled in metal and enameling techniques, Jean's latest passion is working with and teaching workshops in PMC (Precious Metal Clay) and enameling.

See page 179

Eve's Apple pendant: 1½" x 1½" fine silver PMC, tumble burnished except in the crevices, enamel.

Liquid Flux As Etching Resist For Bàsse-Taille
PHYLLIS WALLEN

Phyllis Wallen died September 28, 2000. She had been a noted enamelist in San Diego since the early 1970s. She was involved in the beginnings of the San Diego Enamel Guild.

See page 183

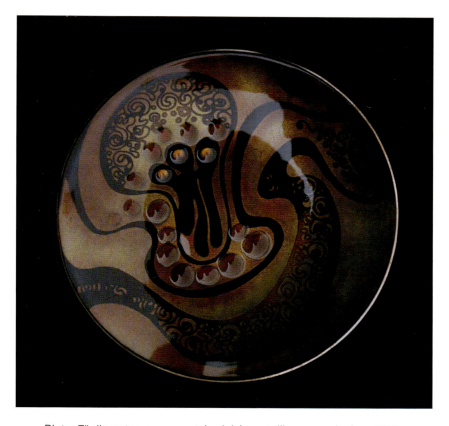

Plate: 7" diameter, copper, etched, bàsse-taille, enamel, circa 1974.

Cloisonné Opaque Enamel Jewelry
Ginny Whitney

Ginny Whitney, like the other professional enamelists in this book, has a curriculum vita too lengthy to print here. She began enameling with Bob Kulicke in 1968 and in the years that followed had many metalsmithing teachers whom she sought out when she needed a certain technique. Some of her enameling knowledge comes from her own experimenting. The patterns and colors of Russian Constructivist work influence her enamels. Color is the starting point and a dominant feature of all her work.   *See page 187*

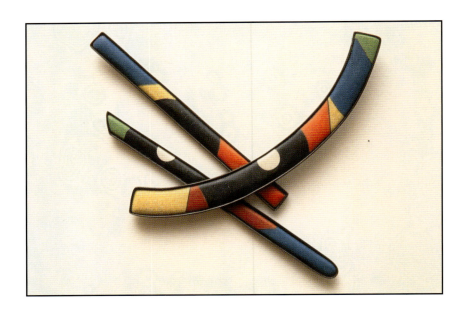

Pin: 3½" x 3¾" x ¼" opaque matte enamel,
sterling and fine silver fabricated setting.

Selected Pieces From The Collection of Lilyan Bachrach

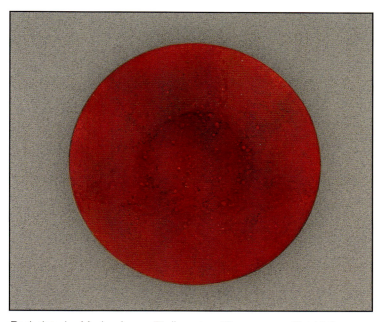

Red plate by Marian Lang. 5" diameter, 18 ga copper. Gold foil covers entire piece under the red transparent enamel.   Photo by J.A. Perry

"Coin for Hironymous" by William Harper. 2" dia. x ½" copper, fine silver wire, reversible, edge hammer thickened. Of enameling interest: some flat wires are used flat.
Photo by J.A. Perry

Champlevé wall piece by Hede von Nagel. 5" dia. enamel, copper, etched, gold plated. Of enameling interest: copper frame fused and welded; not gold plated.   Photo by J.A. Perry

Cloisonné plaque by Joseph Trippetti. 4" x 12", domed copper, fine silver wires. Of enameling interest: the use of 2 or 3 wires close together to appear as a wider line.   Photo by J.A. Perry

Pins by Lilyan Bachrach. (l) Cloisonné pin 1½" dia., 18 ga fine silver, fine silver wire, fabricated sterling frame. (r) Limoges pin 2" dia., 18 ga copper, enamel, silver foil, wet packed.   Photo by J.A. Perry

Three pins by Lilyan Bachrach. (l.) 2½" x 2½" fine silver, fused fine silver wire, frame is fabricated fine silver and sterling. (c.) 2½" x 2" cloisonné, 28 ga copper domed and planished, 24k cloisonné wire, frame is fabricated gold plated sterling. (r.) 2" x 2½" fine silver 28 ga domed, fine silver wires, setting is fabricated sterling.

Photo by J.A. Perry

Door plate by Lilyan Bachrach. 4" x 12", 18 ga copper, fine line black design filled in with overglazes.   Photo by J.A. Perry

Mezuzahs by Lilyan Bachrach. 1" x 5" overglaze painting, fine line black enamel mounted on custom made walnut and cherry cases. Photo by J.A. Perry

Footed bowl by Lilyan Bachrach. 8" x 10" raised 18 ga copper, pewter rim, wet stencil. Design on the outside mirrors the design on the inside.
Photo by J.A. Perry

Orange flower plate by Lilyan Bachrach. 6" diameter, 18 ga copper, overglaze painting, fine line black. Photo by J.A. Perry

Deep Bowl #3 by Lilyan Bachrach. 4½"x 5½" copper, overglaze painting, black enamel inside.
Photo by J.A. Perry

Temple Emanuel Portable Ark by Lilyan Bachrach: Enamel — six 12" steel squares, dry and wet stencil. Wood structure of black walnut, made by Anthony La Rocco. Enameled doors slide apart. The section with enamels lifts off for transporting.

Foils: Fine Silver and 24k Gold
Marianne Hunter

My jewelry incorporates elements of enamel on fine silver or copper. The completed pieces range in size from about 2" x 3" to 16". The copper is 18 ga to 20 ga and the fine silver is 20 ga to 24 ga. I begin each piece with an exact drawing to scale. I need to plan because most of my work is a combination of materials and they all have to fit together. The drawing also allows me to plan for placements of gold and silver foils over and under layers of transparent and opalescent enamels. I only make color drawings for clients; otherwise I see the color in my mind's eye. Each piece is a story I tell myself as I work.

I still use the Trinket kiln, essentially a hot plate, I purchased in 1967. Each enamel piece takes from one to even 30 firings. I first enamel the front of the piece. Generally, I start with Thompson's #124, 80 mesh, leaded, medium black enamel sifted through a piece of silk stocking held in place with a rubber band or binding wire on a small vial. The first layer is a full coverage, slightly thicker at the edges to protect against burning out. This firing is to orange peel to be able to check for flaws and open pits with a file. The subsequent layers are fired just to maturity, being careful not to over fire. I re-sift and re-fire up to four times until I have a base coat that feels just right.

The images are built up in very thin layers of enamel, applied dry by sifting or by laying on with a tiny knife. I use 24k and fine silver foils cut into precise tiny shapes according to the drawings. The foils are placed over parts of previously fired layers and then covered with successive layers of transparents. The enamel piece requires from 12 to 30 firings because of the thin applications of transparents over the foil.

Since I am contact firing the piece on the surface of the Trinket kiln, I put off counter enameling as long as possible until I feel there is a danger of cracking. To counter enamel, I sift a layer of leftover enamels over a brushed on light coat of AAMCO enameling oil. Originally, I used mineral oil and that worked fine. I do not remember why I changed. I use a flat sable brush to apply a light coat of oil under the enamels and the foils. I tap off the excess enamel and fire the piece, right side up on a trivet. If that is the last firing, fine. If not, each successive firing must be on a trivet with appropriate adjustments in timing. If I have forgotten, in the excitement of the piece, to use the trivet and I have to pry the piece loose from the hot plate, I do it as quickly as possible.

The foil is not added until the design cannot proceed without it. After the front base coat is perfect, I may build up 200 mesh white enamel layers in grisaille, which may then be followed by some areas of foil. I use both 24K gold and fine silver thin foil extensively and cut the foil with a #11 Exacto knife blade. I place the foil on either a piece of smooth cardboard or old postcards with tracing paper on top of the foil. It is important to hold the materials taut and to cut away from where you are holding it. For the large areas of foil, ¼" x ¼" or more, I pierce the foil a few times with a sharpened needle; I have forced the eye of the needle into the eraser of a pencil. Too many holes will increase the possibility of tearing the foil. The foils are positioned with oil, dried, fired just to fusing, cooled, and then covered with silver flux. The last firing is the final step for the enamels. Since the layers I use are so thin, any stoning etc. would only remove detail and serve no purpose. The "modeling" of the surface, achieved by the layered building up of the images, is an integral part of the overall feel of most of my work.

The metal jewelry work is individually hand-fabricated and engraved. I use 24K for all the bezels and about 90 per cent of the other soldered decorative appliqués. I use 14K gold and/or sterling silver for the supporting structure and clasps. Most of my bezels are textured with an engraver to reflect light and emphasize the gold color while adding to the overall richness of the piece. When all the sections are finished and assembled, I engrave on the back of the assembled piece my signature, the number of the piece, the date, and the title with a poem.

My best advice? Don't follow rules (except safety ones). Don't follow me or anybody else! Use information for inspiration for your own experimentation. If your work reflects someone other than yourself, you will have fun as a hobbyist, but as an artist you will be wasting your time. Bring your own voice to the song of visual language.

Decals and Ceramic Pencils
June E. Jasen

A decal is a design or picture printed on specially prepared paper for transferring an image to glass, wood and other materials. Developed in the 1700s for the ceramic industry, they were used as an easier and less expensive way to produce and imitate china painting.

The patterns, usually silk-screened, are made into decals with organic oxides, glazes or stains with an inorganic fixative. Books are available that tell you how to make them. I prefer to buy the decals, as it is easier and more cost effective for me to shop at a ceramic hobby and supply store. Hobby ceramic trade shows have vendors who sell them. Factories that produce decals for the porcelain, enamel and glass industries will make the decals you design for a large order.

I alter a decal I buy to make it mine. Starting with a large decal, I cut it up to suit the scale and aesthetic needs of the final enamel piece. For years, I made enamel dresses, which needed a pattern, or a bridal gown, which needed a bridal bouquet. Decals were a perfect solution to be sandwiched between layers of enamel. I created and copyrighted two series: "Interchangeable Dress-Up Dolls" Necklace Series and the "Clothing Pins Series." My pieces range in size from 1" to 24".

I first decide what I want to make, perhaps a bowl or a small pin. I usually have my rough sketches all drawn in my head instead of on paper. I begin with a clean, smooth enameled surface. This base coat surface is necessary for the decal to adhere. First, the piece is annealed in the kiln, and then pickled to remove firescale, rinsed. Both sides are scrubbed with a grease-removing liquid dish detergent and rinsed. I always enamel the back first with 80 mesh hard black enamel. I use unleaded enamels with a variety of sifters: either 80 mesh and then 60 mesh or 100 mesh and then 80 mesh. Sometimes I paint Scalex, a firescale inhibitor, on the front, let it dry and then sift enamel over Klyr-Fyre on the back. When the piece is fired and cool, the Scalex falls off. I file off any firescale on the edge of the piece. Next, the front is scrubbed and rinsed, and I sift on the enamel.

The decal is soaked in a flat, plastic container filled with warm water to loosen it from its backing. The decal should slip off easily. If not, soak it a little more. My water is relatively clean of harsh chemicals so I do not need to use distilled water. Sometimes

I place the decal in the water with the image facing up, which lets me see when the decal lifts from the backing paper, and sometimes I place the decal in the water with the paper side up, to prevent possible excess curling of the decal.

I usually use my fingers instead of tweezers to transfer the decal to the enameled surface. It does not matter if some of the decal hangs over the edge of the piece because you can trim it after it dries. While it is wet, you can move it around, but not excessively. When the decal is in place, the water and air must be removed. Working from the center with a rubber squeegee, a smooth card or a Q-tip, press just hard enough for all the water to move to the edge. Wipe the water away with a tissue or a paper towel. Then place the piece in a dust-free area to dry naturally. If I am in a hurry, I will use either a heat lamp, a warm radiator, or the top of the kiln. When dry, any excess decal is cut away, and the piece is checked for bubbles.

If you see any air bubbles, prick or cut them with a pin or an Exacto knife to release the air and press down the decal in that spot. If the decal is not adhered to the enameled surface, it might not fuse and will not be permanent. The enamel piece, supported on a stilt, is placed in the kiln at 1450°F to 1500°F to remove the film on the decal, which takes from one to four minutes. Depending on the size of the piece, there will be a small pop sound inside the kiln. After the combustion takes place, a fine black, gray or brown film comes from the top of the kiln door and may settle on the surface of the piece. This film will burn away. At this point, avoid the temptation to vent or crash the kiln by opening the door and losing temperature.

After the first stage in which the film burns off, colored dyes and oxides from the decal will bond with the liquefying surface of the enamel. Fusion takes place in this stage. After the piece is removed from the kiln, I check for perfect fusion. To do this, I hold the work under a light source and shift the piece from side to side to see whether the surface is even, reflective and glossy. If not, then the piece is re-fired. If you overfire the decals, they will sink into the enamel. This is particularly true of the reds, which always have a lower fusing time. When bonded to the enameled surface, the decal will appear matte. Any transparent enamel or flux can be fired over the fired decal. There seems to be no limit to the number of layers of transparents or firings for over the decals.

I also use ceramic pencils to create an underlying design element or to put a drawing in place. Ceramic pencils must be applied to a matte surface and then fired. The trick to using pencils is that the surface must have tooth, just like drawing paper has its own rough surface. There are two ways to matte the surface to give it tooth: with an Alundum stone or with matte-salts from a stained glass supply store. Matte-salts come with directions, and the precautions should be followed. After you draw with the ceramic pencils, you can use water to feather out the color, almost like a watercolor. You do not need to cover the surface with enamel, because the matted surface will glaze during the firing process. You must fire these drawings low or you will lose the color.

Sometimes I use lusters as a final coat over the fired enamels. All the ceramic materials that I integrate with my enamels have similar firing temperatures. Some do have a tendency to combust, but everything that one does in the studio with the kiln must be respected or tragedy can befall you. I respect my materials, and they give me fabulous results. I admit that this is only the beginning of what we can learn and apply from the other fire arts. Please continue my search and make beautiful objects to make you proud.

LARGE MOSAIC ENAMELS
JEAN FOSTER JENKINS

An enamel of any size can be produced by working sectionally. I cut copper sheet into irregular shapes to enhance and strengthen a design and to give the illusion of a large single piece. The pieces are mounted on a single sheet of ¾" marine plywood. This method requires a worktable large enough to lay out the full-scale work. I have made many panels by this method, the largest being 5' x 7', which is the size of my worktable. The large panels are hung with the two-piece brackets used for wall cabinets.

I first design a marquette about one-third the size of the planned enamel mosaic. It is an accurate full-color depiction, to scale. Then I make a cartoon (a line drawing) to plan the cutting of the sections of the mosaic and number each piece. The cartoon should be based on the abstract design of your composition and divided into smaller pieces as necessary. Avoid long, thin shapes, C shapes or S shapes and highly irregular shapes. With a pantograph, I enlarge the cartoon to full size on wide butcher paper. I then make any necessary corrections and number the pieces to match the first cartoon. Each piece should be able to fit comfortably in your kiln with a 2" margin on all sides.

I first work on the plywood sheet to which the enameled sections will be attached. Wood sealer is applied to the back and edges of the plywood sheet. When dry, square (¾" to 1") aluminum tubing is cut to form an X shape to be screwed to the back to ensure the rigidity of the panel. Allow clearance for the frame. These aluminum tubing pieces should be drilled to accept wood screws that will go through the tubing and halfway through the plywood. The X shape is positioned on the plywood and screwed in place. The plywood is turned over to accept the tracing of the cartoon and then the copper pieces. The full-scale cartoon is placed on the plywood and fastened in place on two sides with drafting tape. The cartoon, including the numbers, is traced onto the plywood with a fabric marker wheel and carbon paper.

I buy large pieces of 18 ga industrial scrap copper, cold-rolled, annealed if possible. With a Beverly shear, an electric shear or even a jeweler's saw, I cut the copper after I have cleaned it to remove any oil or dirt. The cartoon pieces are glued with rubber cement one at a time to a piece of copper. After the copper is cut to shape, its number is put on the back with an electric engraver. The rubber cement is removed from the back of the cartoon piece and the cartoon piece is saved in a folder for reference. The copper pieces are flattened with a rubber or leather mallet on an anvil.

I clean the metal in a pickle of the standard Sparex solution to remove the copper oxide, rinse well and scour with steel wood and detergent. When the water sheets off the surface, the metal is grease-free. I wear latex or plastic gloves to protect my hands and to protect the metal from fingerprints.

I use primarily leaded enamels from my inventory in 80 mesh and 150 mesh. I use 150 mesh when the piece requires four or more coats. I apply the enamels by either sifting or wet packing and use various techniques depending on my design.

For the base coats, I use liquid hard flux with backing enamel for counter and 80 mesh medium flux sifted over a solution of metho gum on the front. The gum I use is carbo-metho-cellulose (CMC) from Hercules Powder Co., Wilmington, Delaware; 52 grams to make five gallons. To make it into solution, I dissolve all 52 grams in one gallon of distilled water and then mix in another four gallons of distilled water.

Smooth, even coats of counter enamel on the back will discourage warping. The irregular shapes and larger pieces are fired on the "bed-of-nails" stilt. My kilns have a pyrometer and a rheostat. The kiln is preheated to 1550°F before placing the piece in the center of the kiln with small areas or angles nearest to the door, away from the elements. I check the firing by opening the door a crack. After the piece is fired, it is weighted with a press plate on a warm marble slab to keep it flat. The hard fusing enamels are fired first, the opaque reds and oranges added close to the last firing.

After every firing, the loose scale from the edge of the copper piece is removed with a medium-cut metal file. Each piece is placed on the cartoon as I work. For efficiency, I enamel all pieces of the same color first. They are sifted, fired and, when cool, are placed where they belong on the plywood. I plan all the colors initially. Wherever I plan to use silver foil, I sift and fire 80 mesh medium fusing white on that area. The foil is cut and placed on a sheet of static preventative before being positioned with diluted gum; it is fired when dry.

The biggest problem with enameling copper is that the copper grows with each firing. The copper expands in the heat, and the glass solidifies before the copper has returned to its original size. Therefore, I use my cartoon pattern to check the size of each piece. If any edge needs to be ground off, I trace that edge with a permanent marker. I grind as needed and keep each piece its proper size.

My motor has an exhaust hood for an expandable rubber wheel with a coarse (80 grit) wet-or-dry abrasive belt. The wheel is kept wet with a spray bottle of water to prevent heating and dust. I wear a particle mask. I do not grind or stone the enamels for a smooth finish: I feel the irregularities of enamel thickness enhance the visual impact.

When all the pieces have been well developed, I climb a tall stepladder to look down on the work as a whole to see where color value changes are needed. The design grows, as an easel painting would develop. I keep complete notes on each piece of the cartoon pattern.

For indoor installation, I use hot glue to attach the enamel pieces to the plywood. Next, I apply non-sanded grout, formulated for kitchens and bathrooms. Oxides are added to the grout for smooth blending from one section to another. The grout is applied with a small artist's spatula; I clean any excess as I go. As a final step, the grout is covered with grout sealer. The mosaic is then ready for framing and/or installation. The pieces must be set and grouted with mortar if the installation is to be outdoors.

I have focused on the way I work today. Tomorrow may bring a different story, so don't be afraid to be creative.

Enamel Crayons and Watercolors on Steel and Iron
JOHN KILLMASTER

Many years ago I conceived of the idea for enamel crayons. After very much experimentation, Thompson Enamel Company began to manufacture these crayons, and they were a tremendous breakthrough for the artist. The crayons enable the artist to draw with enamel just like drawing on paper. I use them in combination with airbrushed enamel watercolors.

The majority of my enamel art is on steel or enameling iron because both metals hold their shape with minimal distortion when fired. I primarily use steel because it is available where I live in Idaho. Enameling iron, however, is preferable because it is formulated for enameling. I start with pencil or charcoal sketches on paper and then combine enamel crayons and watercolors with an airbrush on an enameled plaque. If the enamel is an 8" x 10" flat plaque, I use a small sketch to refer to as I draw on the base coated plaque with an enamel crayon. If I wish to duplicate the sketch, I project the image on the plaque and draw directly over it, thus retaining the character of the original drawing. For larger repoussé panels, I can begin by projecting the imagery directly on the base metal and tracing the contours of the image with a permanent marking pen or by cutting out the drawing projected on a sheet of paper. The paper cutout is placed on the metal as a template to be traced around with a permanent marking pen.

I use 16 ga or 18 ga steel for flat tiles, for panels with turned edges and for large repoussé works. The iron is usually 16 ga ordered from a catalog. I purchase 20 ga or 22 ga cold-rolled (low carbon) steel locally at metal supply companies and enameling iron by catalog. The thin metal I use for 6" or smaller tiles and for shaped and hammered pieces. The steel, bought in 4' x 10' sheets, is cut with an electric hand shear or a manually operated metal shear. Shaped works are easily made with shears and jewelry saws. The rough edges are filed before hammering and ground coating. As with all enameling, the metal has to be cleaned first. With steel and iron, a special ground coat needs to be applied and fired before the vitreous enamels.

To prepare the metal for enamel ground coating, I first immerse the piece in Sparex 2, formulated to clean off rust from iron and steel. This is not necessary if the metal is new and coated with oil. However, the oil must be cleaned off with soap or detergent until water does not bead up on the metal surface. Cleanser powder is then applied and the surface is scrubbed with a scrub brush or pad and rinsed with hot tap water. The piece is air dried by standing it vertically against a support.

A ground coat for enameling iron and steel is best applied by an automotive touch-up spray gun. Ground coat #16 Thompson enamel requires thinning with water and straining through an 80 mesh screen to eliminate any large particles. The thinning and screening is essential for all material used with a spray gun or an airbrush. A spray booth with an outside exhaust or a fan and table setup out of doors is necessary for all enamel spraying. Care must be taken not to inhale the spray.

For spraying, I use an air compressor with an adjustable regulator providing up to 25 pounds of pressure. The liquid enamel, used with the spray gun, is diluted about half enamel and half tap water and then strained. I fill the cup half full with the diluted enamel and evenly spray a 1/8" layer of ground coating on the back and let it air dry. With a hot air dryer it takes 10 minutes, whereas in the sun it takes 30 minutes. I then spray the front and let it dry. The piece is then ready to be fired in a pre-heated kiln.

I have a 110V kiln that is 12½"w x 12¼"d for small enamels. The door opens horizontally. For larger pieces I have a home-made 230V kiln with a 24" x 26" chamber. The door of this kiln swings down and is counter-balanced with weights and cables. There are fire bricks on the inside floor of the kiln to support firing screens and trivets. Infinite switches, simple to install, provide manual temperature control on both kilns.

The ground coat is fired at 1500°F to maturity. Additional coats of 250 mesh porcelain enamel (the liquid enamel referred to as base color coats) are sprayed over the fired front ground coat, but not as thickly. When planning to use the airbrush, I prefer the base coat to be white. When using an airbrush combined with enamel crayons and enamel watercolor, I also prefer to work on a white base coat. This coat is fired at 1450°F for about three minutes. The length of firing time depends on the size of the piece and the thickness of the metal. Subsequent firings are underfired from 1340°F to 1360°F. I use both the pyrometer and my eye to determine when a piece is ready to be removed from the kiln.

I use the airbrush with the thinned enamel watercolor. Although thinned and screened, porcelain enamel is too coarse for the airbrush. The airbrush I recommend is a dual action, gravity feed with the color cup positioned near the tip above the needle; this one allows easy cleaning and color changing. The airbrush enables an enamelist to produce delicate gradations and extremely subtle shadings of colors and layered overlaps of different colors, approximating art done using watercolor paint. Some practice is necessary to perfect airbrushing.

Enamel watercolor comes in cake form with a water soluble wax binder in it. It is necessary to add drops of water to soften it enough to use with a watercolor brush just like pan watercolor paint. To use enamel watercolor with the airbrush, thin the color with water 1:1, strain it to eliminate any particles and fill the cup half full with color. Begin by adjusting the air-pressure to 12 lbs. PSI and pull back the trigger for air while pressing down to release color. Holding the airbrush away from the surface gives a broad spray, while holding it close creates soft linear effects. Almost any tool can be used to remove unwanted sprayed color. If you remove some of the dried enamel with a tool, you will get a sharp line; if you remove it when wet, the line will be blended.

The crayon colors, especially black, brown and yellow, come through the firing process without losing their richness; other colors lose their intensity, but the result can vary widely depending on the manufacturing process and pigments available at the time. The colors available in both crayons and watercolors are black, brown, blue, orange, yellow, green and red. White is available in crayons, and clear is available in watercolors. I would suggest you make some samples of how the colors fire. Enamel crayon usually fires to a matte surface. To regain a glossy surface you can cover it with a layer of enamel watercolor in a light color or the clear.

To begin an enamel crayon and airbrush art work, I draw with the black, blue or brown crayon. If you find that the glossy surface resists the crayon, a light layer of hairspray adds some texture that aids the adhesion of the crayon. The hairspray will burn away leaving no trace. You can either fire the drawing or develop the image further before firing by combining several colors, by blending or by dissolving lines with water in a watercolor brush. Enamel watercolors need to be applied twice as thick as the intended effect because firing reduces the enamel and diminishes the intensity of the color by one half. Again, experiments are recommended before you attempt a large piece. Enamel watercolor is fired at 1350°F for about 2½ minutes. **Do not overfire!** If you do, you will lose the colors.

I have found enamel crayons and watercolors very freeing, expressive and applicable to a vast range of possibilities when used alone as well as combined with other types of enamels. I use airbrushes, spray gun, paint brushes, shakers, sgraffito tools, silk-screening, alone or in combinations. The possibilities are unlimited!

Champlevé With Ferric Chloride
Audrey Komrad

Champlevé (shahmp-luh-vay), meaning "raised plane" in French, is the process by which a design is cut, gouged or etched out of metal to create low areas for the enamel. After many layers of enamel have been fired, the piece is stoned and may be re-fired to restore a glossy finish. The unenameled metal areas may be waxed, polished or plated. I cut, clean and etch many pieces at one time, but I fire each piece separately. Each piece requires approximately 8 to 10 firings.

Most of my work is either jewelry or small plaques. My jewelry usually ranges from 1½" to 2½" circles or interesting shapes. My plaques range from 4" to 7" circles and squares. I do a detailed drawing before I cut or select the copper piece. In my drawing, the lines for the resist, the unenameled metal, are of various widths. None of the resist lines are narrower than 1/32". Although I do not work out my colors in the drawing, I determine where I want the darks and the lights, where the foils will go and if and where there will be cloisonné wires. I use Vidalon tracing paper to transfer the drawing to the copper after it has been annealed, cleaned and brushed.

The copper sheets I buy are 10 ga, 12 ga and 14 ga. I use a 1/0 or 0 blade in a jeweler's saw to cut the copper. The thicker the copper, the deeper the etch can be. A deeper etch allows for more layers of transparents over the opaques. I often dome the piece but not until the etching is completed. When I make a pendant, I have a "neck" as part of the piece. It will be turned back later to become a loop for the chain. The neck eliminates having to frame the enamel or to solder on a jump ring. I usually use 18 ga x 30 ga fine silver wire.

After the copper shapes are cut, the pieces are annealed. I place a number of pieces on a wire mesh trivet into the kiln at 1500°F. The copper is fired to a reddish glow and then plunged into cold water. Next is pickling in warm Sparex 2 *(follow the directions on the can)* to remove any firescale. Then comes the cleaning of the copper. I use Lea Compound C on a hard, stitched, muslin buff on my polishing machine. When the whole piece is buffed, it is rinsed very well with detergent and water. If you do not have a buffing wheel, a good copper cleaner will do; I like Copper-Glo. The piece is rinsed after buffing but additionally wiped with lighter fluid, rinsed again and dried.

I then transfer my design to the metal with carbon paper as a pattern for the Weber's Liquid Etching Ground that I use as a resist. The resist prevents the metal under it from being etched. If in time it thickens, I thin it with mineral spirits. A border of resist is needed around all the edges. For a small piece of jewelry, paint a border about 1/8" and to 3/16" for a plaque. The border prevents the edge of the enamel from chipping or getting an underbite during the etching. Use a good, fine pointed brush. It is better to go over the lines several times with thin applications until there is no pink copper showing through than to apply the resist too thickly. Let the resist dry. Then, if you wish, you can sgraffito a design in the dried resist but remember that the resist lines should not be narrower than 1/32". If you are a beginner, leave these lines a little wider.

Having removed any resist from the areas that are to be enameled, I let the piece dry overnight before applying Bee's wax, paraffin or candle wax to the back and the edges of the piece. I melt the wax in an old frying pan, keeping the heat low to prevent the wax from smoking. With an old brush that I keep just for waxing, I paint on the wax, being careful not to disturb the resist on the front. The wax will cool and harden fast.

The set-up for the etching is a 14" x 9" x 2" deep Pyrex dish *(never metal)* for six to eight jewelry pieces. If I am etching fewer pieces, I use a smaller dish. A solution in a large container will etch faster than the same amount of solution in a small container because some surrounding air facilitates the etching. I place a row of triangular glass or plastic rods to support the pieces in the dish. I have had the best results with Ferric Chloride, even though nitric acid will etch the copper faster. Ferric Chloride etches by gravity so the pieces are placed **upside down** on the rods. They are supported only on the acid resist border.

The acid solution is poured slowly into the dish until the level of the liquid is just touching the under surface of the piece. That side has the design. The biting action of the solution takes place on the surface of the liquid. From time to time, I stir the solution with a pigeon feather, moving it gently over the surface to remove any bubbles. If you cannot find a feather, a wooden stick will do. Any bubbles trapped on the surface of the copper will retard the etching.

The Ferric Chloride is safer because it does not have dangerous fumes and produces no underbite if used properly. I purchase a 5 pound bottle of the purified lumps. The lumps keep better than either the liquid or the powder. Ferric Chloride does not etch silver.

 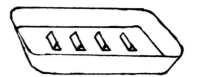 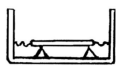

| Pendant with tail to be bent into jump ring. | Paint etching ground in narrow border around the edge. | Plastic triangles set up to support piece | Piece set up face down on etching bath |

The solution I use is 13 oz *(avoirdupois)* Ferric Chloride lumps in two quarts warm water. Put the water in a plastic bucket and add the Ferric lumps. **Caution: Aways add acid to water.** I wear heavy rubber gloves to break up the lumps in the water until they are in solution. Although this acid will not burn your hands like nitric does, it can yellow the skin.

I check the etch occasionally. I have a bowl of water next to the etching dish. Wearing the special rubber gloves, I remove the piece and place it immediately in the bowl of water. Do not allow it to be exposed to the air or a green powder will form, which happens when Ferric solution is exposed to the air. **Important:** if this green powder is heated in a kiln, it forms chlorine gas, which is extremely dangerous to inhale.

While the piece is under the water, the depth of the etch is checked with a stainless metal tool. If you see a bright spot, rub this spot with the tool. These small, round, bright spots mean that an air bubble has been trapped there. The tool will clean the places on the metal where it may not be etching properly. If any of the acid resist lines are lifting up, the piece is placed in a bowl of water with a little ammonia for a few minutes, then into a bowl of clear water. The piece is dried and resist applied where needed. The resist is allowed to dry and then replaced in the Ferric solution. With the solution I use, the etch takes about eight to ten hours. I usually start it early in the morning to be able to check it throughout the day. I etch several pieces at a time, but if I etch only one piece, the time will be shorter. It is always better to do a long, slow etch to avoid underbite. Underbite is when the sidewall of the etched area becomes uneven.

When the solution turns murky green it is exhausted. Remove the pieces and place them in a bowl of water while you replace the solution. To dispose of the acid solution, I neutralize it with a little ammonia in another container and pour it into a small hole I dig in the corner of my backyard.

To do multiple bites, having different levels, I make the first bite about one third of the total thickness of the metal. The second and third bites together should go down no more than two thirds of the total thickness of the metal if you are using 10 ga or 12 ga. If the copper is 14 ga, do not etch down more than halfway for total bites because then the metal will be too weak. If I want other shallower etching areas, I scratch away some of the resist when the etching is about halfway done. You can repeat this after another few hours. I use a piece of 18 x 30 flat cloisonné wire to test the depth of the etch. The multiple bites in foil areas will make the foil appear to float.

After the etching is completed, wash each piece in water and soak in ammonia for 10 minutes, then rinse very well. I remove the etching ground with either paint thinner or turpentine. The wax is removed by heating the piece gently in another old, shallow frying pan. Some of the etching ground can be removed with this method also. When all the resist and wax have been removed, the metal is scrubbed with an old toothbrush and a mixture of hot water, detergent and a little ammonia. After being rinsed very well with running water, the work is pickled in warm Sparex 2 solution for 15 minutes, washed well and dried. If I want to dome a piece, I anneal it as before and then use a sandbag followed by a metal mushroom stake and a rawhide mallet.

Next I drill any holes that will be needed. If I have left a neck for a pendant, I turn it back into a loop for a chain. Finally, the piece is rubbed with an 8" brass brush until the metal is shiny. It is then rinsed well and ready to be enameled. If you are not enameling immediately, wrap the polished metal in paper towels.

I use 80 mesh leaded, mostly medium fusing enamels and some soft fusing enamels. I wash small amounts of enamel, usually enough for a day's work. The enamels are washed about 10 times with tap water and then twice with distilled water. For wet inlaying, I use a 00 or 000 pointed sable brush. With distilled water, I wet inlay all colors thinly to avoid trapping air that will cause pits. In the deeper etched areas, I often use a light opaque under the transparents. To keep the color bright, I use a lighter transparent under a deeper transparent. If I need to lighten a transparent color, I mix flux with it. If you use opaques alone, put them into the narrow areas and use transparents for the larger areas where more light can enter. I generally fire at a little under 1450°F to orange peel stage, except for the final firing which is to maturity.

I fire the base coats in two firings, the back first with the front protected with Scalex, a firescale inhibitor. Keep a separate brush for the Scalex. Using a color compatible with the front color scheme, I do three light siftings on the back using Klyr-Fyre diluted 1/3 to 2/3 water. When dry, the piece is fired to orange peel and cooled. The Scalex is washed off. If some of it remains, use a stiff toothbrush, a glass brush or a dental tool to remove the last of it. The piece is pickled in warm Sparex 2 solution for about ten minutes, rinsed and dried. Then I brass brush the front of the piece until shiny and rinse again. On the front, I do two very light siftings of medium fusing flux, spraying between siftings with the Klyr-Fyre solution. A little of the pink copper may show through. Fluxing over the entire front of the piece prevents the buildup of a heavy coat of firescale in the subsequent firings. This coat of flux will be stoned off later where the copper is to be bare.

The deepest and largest areas that are to have foil or cloisonné wires are set up first. The deepest areas to have only foil receive one or two additional layers and give the foil a floating effect. I cut the foil between tracing paper with small, sharp, pointed scissors. I like the foils cut small or finely minced. Paper punches work well, too. To position the foil, I use a small pointed brush with distilled water that has a drop of Klyr-Fyre. Firescale on the walls of a cell can destroy the edges of silver foil. To prevent that, a thin coat of either a light color, medium fusing, washed opaque or flux is wet packed on the cell walls with water and fired before setting in the foil. Firescale does not affect gold foil. I have found that repeated firings of warm colors over silver foil sometimes produce undesirable changes in the color of the transparents. Finally, all the areas are enameled in thin-fired layers until the enamel in the cells are slightly higher than the bare copper. The final firing is to maturity.

You have a choice for the enamel finish: matte, semi-gloss or high-gloss. A matte finish is my favorite. It is a long process. I use Alundum stones in 150 and 220 grits. They are about 6" long and 1" thick. The 150 grit comes in a smaller size and is good for small, hard to reach areas. Under running water, I start with the 150 grit and stone in all directions. When the unenameled copper areas are almost clean, I move to a 220 grit or the fine side of a Carborundum stone. During the stoning, you need to check for low spots or pits in the enamel. If there are any, you need to clean the piece before adding enamel. I scrub the surface with a glass brush, soak the piece in a solution of detergent, ammonia and water for a few minutes and rinse thoroughly before I reapply and fire the enamel where needed. Then I continue the stoning process until the entire surface is smooth and dull. There will be a lot of scratches at this point. Next come wet and dry emery papers to remove the scratches. I use 220, 320, 400 and 600 grits. I cut them into 4" and 6" squares that I use over a block of wood. I start with 220 grit then go to the others, rubbing in one direction over the piece and then in the opposite direction. Each step removes the previous scratches. It is best not to rush through the stoning.

When all the scratches are out, I wash the piece with detergent, ammonia and water again, rinse and dry. At this point, I use a polishing machine. My machine has two spindles, ½ hp, 3450 rpm with a sealed motor and filter. For polishing, I first use a bobbing compound on a hard-sewn muslin buff; then I wash and dry the piece and go to a hard-sewn felt buffing wheel with tripoli. The next step is to polish with a soft felt wheel and red rouge followed by a soft chamois wheel. These polishing steps can also be done with a flexible shaft.

After the piece is polished, I wrap it in a soft cloth until I send it to be gold plated. The plater applies a coat of nickel before the gold plating which helps the gold plating last longer. The appearance of the final piece depends on how good a job you did with the stoning and the buffing of the metal. Take your time and you will be rewarded with a beautiful surface and a sensuous enamel.

Portrait With Enamel Watercolors
ORA K. KULLER

My design for a portrait in enamel is based on either a photocopy of a photograph or my sketch of the subject. The work is divided into small sections of various sizes and shapes. Each piece is an almost independent unit. Cutouts made from photocopies of the design are used for cutting the metal, blocking the area, transferring designs and shapes, etc.

18 ga copper or fine silver is used for parts that are fired many times. Less complicated sections are made of 20 ga metal and for tiny pieces that will be fired just three to four times, 22 ga or even 24 ga will suffice. I use a frame saw with a 2/0 blade to cut 18 ga metal and a 4/0 or 6/0 for thinner metal and very intricate designs. The metal is first covered with a layer of masking tape, then a layer of double-faced tape. The third layer is the pattern for cutting. After cutting the metal, the layers can be peeled off together and saved. Should a need arise, the pattern is ready to be placed on a fresh piece of metal and re-cut. Holes are drilled in the metal if it is to be connected with screws or other connecting elements. The metal must be cleaned before it is enameled. Annealing in the kiln cleans fine silver, but I heat the copper in a 1500°F kiln till it turns gray green and then clean it with Penny-Brite.

All of my enamels are from Thompson Enamel Inc. I purchase their unleaded 80 mesh enamels and use #533 White Liquid Form enamel as counter enamel on the back of all the segments. This liquid enamel should be the consistency of thin yogurt. It can be poured over the metal or applied with a soft brush. When the counter enamel is dry, I sift enamel on the front.

Sifting the enamel, without any adhesives, through different mesh sifters helps to create a perfect surface for painting. The first sifting of a pale color enamel, like #1202 Off White, is done through a 60 mesh sifter over the whole area of the head, followed by a thin layer of #1202 through a 100 mesh sifter. A last sifting of the #1202 through a 200 mesh sifter is over the whole area, with particular attention to the edges. The tiny grains from the 200 mesh cling better to the edges than the bigger grains and will prevent the edges from burning out. The piece is fired at 1500°F for about 1½ minutes or until the enamel, inside the kiln, looks even and glossy. Removed from the kiln and cooled, the piece is stoned under water with 150 and 200 Alundum stones to ensure a flat surface. In painting a portrait, mounds and hills in the enamel can distort the expression of the face.

Sometimes I sift #1010 White only on the face and neck using a paper cutout to block the hair section. After removing the paper cutout, I paint the bare copper with Scalex leaving a narrow space between it and the sifted enamel. When the Scalex dries, the piece is fired until the enamel is shiny. When cool, the Scalex and the firescale are removed and the bare copper cleaned.

The hair section is painted with a very thin layer of oil base P-3 Black Underglaze and dried on top of the kiln. When dry, the pattern of the hair is sgraffitoed with a metal or wood scriber. Masking the white enamel of the face with the appropriate paper cutout, I sift 200 mesh granules of transparent enamel over the design of the hair and fire the piece until the enamel is shiny and transparent. P-3 Black Underglaze should always be fired with transparent enamel over it.

At this stage, I turn the piece over and sift over the fired counter enamel the same enamel that was sifted on the front. Using the same enamel on the front and on the back reduces the risk of cracks in the enamel.

The features of the face can be drawn free hand, but sometimes I use a copy of my drawing to transfer the outline of the facial features. I make a carbon paper that will be harmless to the enamel surface: Over the flame of a candle I hold a white china plate at an angle that will allow the flame to cover the plate with black soot. I wipe off the soot with a cotton ball and transfer the soot to the back of the portrait cutout pattern. The lines of the design can be traced by placing the blackened side of the drawing on top of the enamel. The transferred lines will appear on the enamel surface very faintly and will give a hint of the correct positions. The next step is painting with the watercolors.

The watercolors come in powder form. The three kinds that I use are Ceramic Pigments, Overglaze Painting Color and the 400 mesh fines of the enamels. Ceramic Pigments are not enamels and will not fire to perfection without an enamel addition of either PF-1 Painting Flux or 913E Mixing White. When mixed with Painting Flux, the colors retain their intensity whereas when mixed with Mixing White, they become lighter and softer. The ceramic pigment and the Mixing White or the Painting Flux are mixed 1 part pigment to 4 parts of either the white or the flux. As I mix the colors I add one to two drops of Klyr-Fyre and a few drops of distilled water, just enough to achieve a good consistency for drawing and painting. The mixture should be smooth and silky because lumps do not fire well or fire with a different intensity of color. If these mixtures are kept dust free, they can be used for a few months. Since some of the enamel watercolors and pigments look very different before and after firing, I have one sampler of the colors mixed with the Painting Flux and another with the Mixing White.

With the outline of the features traced on the enamel, I go over the lines with the enamel watercolor. Dipping a 20/0 brush in the darkest color combination that I have, I render thin and delicate lines. The color I use is a mixture of dark brown and dark blue. Drawing with these enamels is not like working with regular watercolor paints. The enamel surface is non-porous, and if I cross over my painted lines, the lines underneath might disappear. The colors dry very quickly and become powdery, and so I have to be very careful not to drag lumps of powder with my brush. On the other hand, I can improve the drawing with ease. With a moist brush the lines can be refined until they are as thin as a hair. I can shape and reshape the drawing until I am content.

The piece is fired at 1450-1500°F for about 1 minute and 20 seconds, or until the lines become darker inside the kiln. Before firing again, a fair amount of work can be done. The shadows can be defined, dark values can be enhanced and the lighter areas can be softened. The addition of Klyr-Fyre to the color makes the paint adhere better to the enamel surface and more layers can be added without disturbing the unfired layers below. As enamel colors tend to be lighter before the firing and darker after, the shadows and lights over the face and neck may be too contrasting. Layers of Mixing White will soften the harsh shadows, and at the same time, if I want, I can add skin color to the portrait.

For a skin color over a base coat of #1010 White, I mix the tiniest amount of OC-70 red, OC-32 Yellow, 1715P-Clover Pink and a larger amount of Mixing White. If the base color is Off White, I use browns for skin color, OC-82, OC-83, OC-85, a little 906E Green and OC-95 blue. The lips are drawn with OC-70 Red and OC-71 Orange. A hint of blue will enhance the white of the eyes. Often during the many firings, the lips will need another application of color. A portrait can require 20 or more firings. It is a slow procedure that requires patience.

During the intermediate steps of drawing and painting the portrait, I take care to fire the piece only imperfectly, otherwise by the fourth or fifth firing the lines and colors may have vanished or been distorted. Enamel watercolors are very delicate and do not tolerate high or prolonged firing. Only when I sense that the piece is nearly perfect will I paint the whole appropriate areas with a thin layer of the skin color mixture and fire a little longer. Delicate details can be added just before the piece is fired to perfection. I employ various techniques and colors to create the design that surrounds the portrait.

I usually connect the enameled pieces to a wood panel with Silicon II. I also use tiny nails that I make from fine silver or copper to hold the enameled pieces in place. I feel the nails echo and enhance the design. When all the pieces are glued to the board, these elements are threaded through the previously made holes to the supporting wood panel. They also add mechanical strength to the work. Finding or making a frame that will compliment the work without competing with it is the last step.

Torch Firing
Deborah Lozier

Torch firing is a wonderful way to experience enameling in all of it stages. I see it as an extension to kiln fired enamels and not a replacement since the results are very different. It requires working from instinct with a sensitive observation of cause and effect. The torch oxidizes and blends the pigments, creates patterns and causes chemical reactions that do not occur with kiln firing. Firing times are intuitive and the temperature is controlled by the length of the flame. The torch fires with a cascade of heat, allowing for control over heat placement throughout the piece. Solder seams and delicate colors (soft enamels) thus can be avoided while areas needing high heat can be hit directly.

This flexibility requires active participation to not overheat delicate areas and to adequately heat the harder enamels. The torch, creating an active heat, causes the enamel to move while the fuel oxidizes the pigments and in turn mixes with the oxides contained in the metal. In thin applications, transparents will shimmer and opaques will take on varying degrees of translucency with glaze-like qualities. In thicker applications, they will become stronger and appear like stone inlay. The more direct contact with the flame, the more exaggerated these effects become.

Heating the piece from underneath creates effects closer to kiln firing, but also limits size potentials. The workable size depends on the heat available from the torch instead of the perimeter of the kiln. I always experiment with the direct flame in mind since color variables differ greatly. Torch firing does have its limits, but also offers possibilities that give a spontaneous and open approach to a historically reserved discipline.

TOOLS and MATERIALS

Eyewear is the most important element for safety. I use Auralens glasses, made for glass blowers, and can be ordered with a prescription. They cost around $180, but provide protection from ultraviolet light, infrared light and sodium flare while allowing good visibility. I use them even for soldering. I also wear leather gloves, an apron and close-fitting natural fiber clothing (no polyester, no sandals). My firing station is equipped with a roof mounted ventilator to remove fumes. No flammable items, such as papers or cloths, are near the firing area.

A good beginning torch set-up is a Smith or Presto-lite acetylene atmosphere regulated torch. Get the B tank not the little mc. The #2 torch will be used the most, but buy as many different tip sizes as you can afford. Oxygen/acetylene is too hot. The little butane hand torches are not hot enough, but if you own them, try them. My top torch recommendation is natural gas and oxygen if you are experienced at using torches. I have two torches with a variety of tips: the National Hand Torch and the Unecon Hand Torch. The Unecon has an automatic shut-off lever. The tips are interchangeable. They can both be used with propane and oxygen. They were bought from Wale Apparatus Company, a glassworking supplier. Smith also makes a nice set-up.

Small to medium scale torch firing set-up and props.
Photo by Deborah Lozier

The basic #1 to #5 silver-smithing tips are good for jewelry scale pieces. For larger scale pieces I use Wale's hush tip that comes in three sizes. These tips create a bushy rather than a focused flame and they are good for heating a general area. Smith offers a tip, called a high heat tip, which should offer similar results.

Many of my firings require two torches. I use an automatic striker to light the torch with one hand. When two torches are being used, the torch hook and automatic shut-off lever become important. For safe two torch firings, I have bench hooks to hold the torches. Having two large torches going with the ability to turn one of them off quickly is safer. Obviously, limit yourself to one torch until you are experienced before trying to use two at once. Until then, use an assistant to handle the second torch.

The firing station is fairly simple. I use a tripod, a ring stand, a rotating annealing pan, three-point-open-bottom trivets, and open weave stainless steel screens. The screen of 18 ga to 20 ga wire and woven at least ¼" apart is available from many suppliers. I modify soup cans to create trivet stands and use an annealing pan so I can rotate the piece during firing. I use large steel bolts and washers to raise up the tiny trivets when I am firing rings. Steel rods can be bent into holders and stands for odd shaped pieces. The stainless steel screen, on a tripod or ring stand, works for smaller pieces that are not enameled on the back, such as an earring or pin. I attach 18-20 ga steel binding wire to create a simple, non-stick lift for small pieces enameled on all sides. Very small pieces can be held directly with a pair of holding tweezers if the pieces have a secure appendage to grasp. I also use props sold for cooking over campfires and home barbecues along with a variety of household items that I alter to meet the need. The firing solutions are an important part of the designing process and require constant modifications.

I use all Thompson's unleaded enamels except for their five C-grade transparents, which cast a gray blue haze across the surface unless they are only fired from underneath. Leaded enamels are unsuitable because the lead tends to rise to the surface as a gray haze. I originally used just the 80 mesh, but I now screen the 80 mesh enamels to have the 325 mesh for painting and intricate champlevé and the 200 mesh for a more even sifting. Many of the liquid enamels are appropriate for torch firing but respond best to a natural gas and oxygen torch set-up. Their fine grains and thin applications make them susceptible to oxidation and burning away.

Any metal that can be enameled in a kiln can also be torch fired. I prefer working with copper or fine silver. Copper has a lively color personality of its own and a high melting point, which allows flexibility for heat placement. I do not wash the enamels, but I do try to keep the work area clean. The application tools and procedures are basically the same as kiln firing. I clean the base metal, use enamel adhesive for sifting and wet techniques, allow the piece to dry and then apply heat. All the techniques can be incorporated, realizing that torch firing creates different color qualities. Beautiful abstract surfaces can be achieved. The uneven heat and contaminates in the fuel will not produce the pure color and density found in contemporary cloisonné work. Plique-à-jour is not an option as there is not enough metal surface area. With the torch, the enamel and oxides move with the heat, which causes lines to blend and colors to flow.

FIRING and DESIGN

The main difference in designing for torch firing lies in creating areas for direct torch access. In its powdered state, the enamel will burn with direct contact with the flame. For color clarity and proper fusing, the enamel initially requires indirect heat from the metal. This means there must always be an available area of bare metal or previously fired enamel to start the torch firing process. If the entire surface of a piece is to be enameled, it must be treated as if it has a front and a back or an inside and an outside, then fired in succession, always leaving a place for the initial torch heat.

For example, if I am firing a bowl, I first apply enamel to the inside of the bowl and direct the flame to the bare metal on the outside. For the next firing, I apply enamel to the outside and direct the flame onto the fired enamel on the inside. I continue to rotate the applications and firings until the piece is complete. I usually do this loosely, with two or three firings in a row on the inside, then moving on to the outside for a few firings. I rinse the piece in water between firings and do not pickle it unless there is an unenameled area from a previous firing that I want free of oxides for a transparent layer.

I plan applying the hard enamels first and in areas that will receive a lot of direct heat while the softer enamels are built up slowly or placed in sheltered areas of the design. Most colors will change with each heating. Many colors improve with increased firings. It takes experience to learn which ones. Color quality will be best if pieces are fired rather quickly. This requires an active and mindful maximize-the-heat technique somewhat similar to soldering. The fusing will follow the heat. The heat will be greatest any time the torch can be placed perpendicular to the surface. I use a bushy flame as for annealing. After the enamel is applied and dry, I begin fusing by heating either a bare metal area or a previously fired enamel layer. With a relaxed spiral rhythm, I gather the heat in an area to start the fusing process. Once an area begins to respond, I focus the heat on that area and then expand it by spiraling the flame throughout the piece. On something small, the response will happen quickly and easily. I can choose to finish the fusion from underneath, or decide to transfer the flame onto the enamel surface to finish the firing.

Large hollow forms will require: two torches, a more acute observation of the fusing taking place and flame contact over the entire surface of the work. Once the fusion begins, I move one of the torches to follow the fusion as it spreads and use the other torch to retain an overall constant temperature. At any scale, a consistent temperature is desired — not too hot, not too cool. Be your own thermostat by moving the torch flame away from the piece periodically so that overheating does not occur.

Heating is also dependent on other variables, including the shape of the piece, the gauge of the metal and the type of trivet or stand it is resting on. A 24 ga pair of earrings, resting on a 16 ga wire screen, will fire easily, using a small to medium soldering flame, in a minute or two. In contrast, an 18 ga bowl resting on a trivet may take more than five minutes with two torches going.

Complete heating is a problem with hollow forms, especially those with a large enclosed volume, and causes some size restrictions. I use a temporary covering for the initial phase of firing to help contain the heat. A tin can with a small window cut out for viewing, resolves the problem for small hollow forms, and a structure can easily be fabricated out of ductwork parts or stainless steel sheet for larger work. Once the enamel begins to fuse, I remove the cover with tongs for complete torch access. When two torches are being used, the torch hook and automatic shut-off lever become important. The tools and firing set-up must be carefully maintained and respected for safe operations. Safety should always come first. The number of firings is piece specific and subjective. More firings usually allow for color depth and intrigue. On an average, I fire pieces 8 to 12 times to orchestrate harmony in the color ranges. As I said before, you need to experiment. There are a few opaques and transparents that are not compatible due to the differences in expansion and contraction. The different fuels create color differences that are more pronounced when the flame has direct contact with the enamel. Transparents will shimmer and clear with intense heat; opaques oxidize more noticeably and many require more thoughtful planning. A clean yellow or orange can be hard to achieve, but if you apply these colors in areas protected from the direct flame, adding oxides to pump up the pigment content, or apply them at the end of the firing sequences it will help. Transparents layered over opaques can protect the opaques from adverse effects and usually improve the intensity and depth of all colors.

The thickness of the layers also affects the color quality. The Thompson #533 liquid white, when hit with a direct flame, creates an incredible rusty orange and beige surface, while this same heat on a thin layer of green or yellow turns dark and unappealing. As the layers are built up, this effect lessens. The copper can also have a first layer of flux to keep the metal oxides from interacting and darkening the color. Keep in mind that transparents tend to become more brilliant with increased firings, even if no fresh enamel is applied, and opaques will weather and fade. You need to plan ahead once you have learned the traits and needs of the individual enamel colors so that colors needing high heat can receive it and those needing a delicate touch can be in protected areas or receive a final light heating. I keep notes of my observations and find them an essential tool.

I solder pieces to construct an object and then enamel it. Torch firing the enamel, when done carefully, can protect the seams from opening. I usually use hard solder and occasionally medium solder. Since solder will flow when heated to its specific temperature, it is necessary to pay attention to the seams and resist applying too much heat to them. If I choose to apply enamel next to a soldered seam, I direct the heat to the seam last and gently pull the torch back to a cooler point of the flame and stop firing just as the enamel is fused, but not a second longer. A lap seam will fare better than a butt seam because it provides more surface area for the solder and allows a little movement without failing. Edges can be rolled over seams or rivets can be added to strengthen them. Many forms can be easily constructed using box making techniques or die forming, all creating very durable connections.

I design appendages with extra surface area for the solder or design them into the body of the piece. I never rest the weight of a piece on an added element during the firing because that would risk pulling the seam apart. I rarely solder after enameling. I have now begun to weld seams for large pieces rather than solder them. The welded seam can be covered with enamel. The seam is not as crisp. Tack welding can also be used with soldering to secure a long seam and maintain a crisp joint line.

FINAL THOUGHTS

I listen to the material's natural potential and set up the work to encourage these natural tendencies to happen and with more predictability. There is control, but I leave a wide margin for error and do allow some of the errors to remain. My working methods are based on the assumption that an accident that can be recreated turns into a technique. The space between the action and the reaction is where discoveries are made, and I work with open eyes to be ready for their arrival.

Vessel Forms
Sarah Perkins

I consider vessels my most important work, but I also make jewelry and utensils. I usually have sketches and color studies of a piece before I start unless it is one in a series that are all similar and I can envision it easily. I do not do detailed drawings because then there would be little to keep me interested in the piece while making it.

My vessels range in size up to 9" tall, which is the largest dimension my kiln can handle. I have 2 kilns: one is 8"w x 10"d x 10"h on a 110V line; the other is 12"w x 14"d x 12"h on a 220V line. I prefer kilns that are deeper than they are wide because the heat is more even farther away from the door. A 220V line recovers faster, which is important when firing larger pieces. I never let the kiln go below 1350°F because the metal could oxidize too much before the enamel flows and cause the enamel to adhere to the oxide layer, which does not stick to the metal and will chip off or peel back. Even in later firings, the enamel always cracks when put in the kiln and needs to have the temperature recover quickly so that the enamel can heal properly.

I use primarily fine silver or copper for vessel forms. The larger pieces are 18 ga or 20 ga; smaller vessels are 20 ga to 22 ga. I would make a 5"d x 5"h bowl of 20 ga fine silver. However, if there were to be soldered additions to the bowl, I probably would make it of 22 ga. I do not clean my metal first unless it has blobs of crud on it, which I just brush or wash off. If I am using transparents throughout, I remove any scratches with a burnisher. It is easiest to enamel on seamless copper or fine silver forms, which means that you must either raise or spin the metal form. Of course, you can buy simple spun forms in copper and alter them. If I want to alter the shape of the vessel I do it before I attach a rim and/or a base.

It is also possible to enamel a seamed piece; but as enamel does not adhere well to solder, the seam must get special attention and is a complication. The three ways I deal with a seam are by: soldering a square wire over the seam, the thickness of the wire being the same as the finished depth of the enamel; covering a clean butted seam with standard metal foil over which I enamel; or using a high lead content enamel as a base coat over the seam.

It is helpful to have attached rims and bases to rest the vessels on when firing them in the kiln. The rims also protect the enamel edge and give the piece a finished look. To solder on a protective rim, it is advisable to have it form an overhang on both the inside and the outside of the piece. To ease fitting and soldering, I make the rim wider than necessary and trim it later.

When soldering fine silver to fine silver, I use hard or IT solder with a high temperature white paste flux containing fluorides, such as Handy Flux. This flux gives off toxic fumes and should be used in a well-ventilated area. Unfortunately, the safer fluxes do not work at these temperatures. When soldering copper to copper, or copper to silver with IT, mix about half-and-half Handy Flux and black flux (available from Indian Jewelry Supply or many welding supply stores). You can use straight black flux, but it is opaque when active and hard to see when the solder flows. If you keep heating to try to force it to flow after the seam is dirty, the copper and silver will fuse instead of becoming soldered. Once this fusing process has begun, it will continue each time the piece is heated and cause the silver to "disappear" by alloying with the copper. Enamel will also tend to pop off the alloy because the metal moves every time it is fired.

Any soldered joint will be subject to eventual break down in the enameling process. With IT solder the break down is very much slower than with hard solder. It is possible to successfully complete a piece with multiple firings using hard solder on unstressed joints, but care must be taken not to overfire the piece, which will cause the solder to break down and endanger the enamel around it.

If I am attaching heavy cloisonné wire or other fairly large metal elements to the surface, I usually tack them in place. Large or heavy pieces are difficult to get to stay on a steep wall with only enamel holding them in place. After the soldering is completed and all the excess solder removed, the piece is pickled and then rinsed in water and baking soda to neutralize the pickle. This rinsing is essential for any piece of metal that has been in pickle otherwise the enamel will be bubbly and porous.

I mostly use 80 mesh, medium or hard, old Thompson leaded enamels, but the Japanese leaded enamels are wonderful. I order these when I need to replace old colors. I do not clean the enamels, but I do use different mesh sizes depending on the application, which generally takes care of cloudy transparents. I am careful not to apply transparents thickly, or if I need a thick coat, to sift out all but the larger grains. If I find some transparents that have been improperly stored and fire cloudy or foamy, I will sift and then wash them. To wet pack I use 3/0 or 4/0 brushes or a wire tool. The sifters I use I make with various meshes of stainless steel screening and plastic containers. I melt the plastic onto the screening with a warm to hot spatula. I find that the sifters you can buy break easily and are too shallow. For sifting on the enamels, I first spray on 1:1 diluted Klyr-Fyre with an airbrush and then use a variety of mesh sizes, mostly I use 80 mesh and 200 mesh enamels.

I begin enameling on the area that will be the hardest to reach for stoning because the enamel flattens a little each time it is fired. Usually this area is the inside of a vessel. If the vessel is a bottle shape, I pour in diluted 1:3 Klyr-Fyre, roll it around and dump out the excess. Then I pour in dry enamel, roll it around and pour out the excess. The piece is dried and fired to maturity. Sometimes I put a dab of enamel on the outside in order to tell when it is fired. The inside will take a little longer firing than the sample on the outside, so it needs a few extra seconds. If there are bare spots after this firing, then I wet pack over them and re-fire, repeating until the whole inside is covered.

If the piece is more open but the walls are fairly high and steep, I usually wet pack the inside with 80 mesh enamel and 1:4 diluted Klyr-Fyre. For this shape, I wet pack the enamel in 3" bands leaving a narrow bare line between each band. This line will prevent the weight of the enamel at the bottom from pulling the enamel nearer the top down into a pile at the bottom. Two or three coats are needed on the inside, so the bands of enamel are staggered if there is bare metal to cover. If the piece is open and shallow, then the Klyr-Fyre is diluted with water to 1:6 solution.

The outside is enameled by whatever method you want to use. After one or two complete coats have been fired on both sides, I trim the overhang of the rim on the side I enameled first. This prevents the enamel on that side from pooling around the rim and becoming too thick if most of the later firings are done with the piece upside down.

If I am going to embed cloisonné wire, I apply the base coat and fire it three times to harden it. After I cut and shape the wires and set the vessel horizontally on a firing support, I place the wires on that section with uncut Klyr-Fyre or wetted Japanese lotus root powder, let it dry and then fire the wires into the enamel. The piece is rotated until all the wires are embedded. Any unwanted scars that remain from the firing points are later cleaned and enameled.

From this point on, enameling a vessel has about the same demands and possibilities as enameling a flat surface. The only difficult part is achieving a consistent underfired surface since the part of the vessel in the back of the kiln tends to fire faster. The enamel is stoned, the uncut overlap of the rim is trimmed, and a final finish is put on the metal just before the last firing.

Cloisonné on Fine Silver with 24k Wires
Merry-Lee Rae

Since 1976, I have been designing and making cloisonné jewelry, ranging from ½" to 2". My method of working is primarily the result of trial and error. After thousands of pieces and as many mistakes, I now have a narrow but proven approach. Each piece is started with a detailed drawing, including the plans for any goldsmithing and gemstones. My color test plates are used to select the enamels I will use. Progress notes are kept as a journal to note any unexpected variations from the firing. If there are any technical difficulties, my notes from other pieces often help to find the cause.

My kiln is a "Firemaster" with a 9"w x 6½"h x 11"d chamber. To reduce drafts in the kiln, the peephole is covered with mica to reduce the drafts. The mica is held in place with masking tape. I rely on the pyrometer. I fire the enamel piece on a stainless steel trivet on a small firing rack. When firing, I wear welder's glasses to protect my eyes and a welder's glove and copper tongs to place the work in the kiln.

The shape is usually cut of 26 ga fine silver from the drawing and domed either with a Bonny Doon Hydraulic Press or by hand in a wooden dapping block. For most designs, I polish the front surface with white diamond tripoli, clean ultrasonically in non-sudsy ammonia and then brass brush with detergent under running water.

I use 80 mesh Thompson or Japanese leaded transparent enamels. The enamels are washed in small quantities with distilled water in a glass, stirring with plastic spoons and a glass stirring rod. The base coat on the front is Thompson's old flux for silver, #1209 or #757. When my supply is gone, I shall have to figure out something else. I spray the piece with a 1:2 solution of Klyr-Fyre and distilled water before sifting. This flux base coat is a very lightly sifted one that barely covers and is fired on a trivet at 1500°F for 70 seconds or until smooth. I try not to look in the kiln before the time is complete. Then on the back, a light to medium color of transparent blue is used because it holds up well and enables me to see variations in the thickness of the counter enamel. The back receives two to three heavy applications. The piece is then ready for the cloisons.

In general, my cloisonné wire is .003 x .060 24k yellow gold that I roll down from .005 x .050 wire. With tweezers and my fingers, I bend the wires, cut them and place them in position on the piece with uncut Klyr-Fyre. When it is dry, the piece is fired to embed the wires in the base coat of enamel. I carefully inspect each wire to be certain that all my partitions have remained in place and that each joint is tight so that one color will not bleed into an adjoining cell.

When the wire design is embedded in the flux base coat, the piece is placed on a Pyrex lid, which ensures a clean surface and allows me to rotate the piece without touching it. The lid also gives a slippery surface to slide the piece easily to the edge and transfer it to a trivet. I use plastic spoons to hold the washed enamels and I wet pack them with a fine brush and dental tools.

I achieve depth and subtle shading by firing many layers of enamel. Most pieces average from 10 to 20 firings. The majority of my shading is accomplished in the first five layers; any subsequent enameling helps to fine tune and bring all cells to the upper edge of the cloisonné wire.

When the enameling is complete, the finishing starts with lapidary equipment to grind the surface of the enamel. The equipment comes setup with a water hose and catch basin. The enamel piece is stuck to a dop stick to make it easy to hold against the wheel. To do this, I warm the enamel piece by placing it face down on top of my kiln and then I heat the dop wax in a small metal pot. Some warm wax is gathered on one end of a short wooden dowel. This wax end is placed on the back of the enamel piece. I now have a little handle to hold on to during the grinding. Be careful not to drip any wax on yourself or on anything that will go into the kiln. The front surface of the enamel piece should be free of any wax.

My lapidary grinder has an 8" expandable drum. The sanding belt I now use is a 40MIC Microfinishing made by 3M, although for years I successfully used a 320 grit Carborundum belt. The equipment comes with a watering system because the process needs to be done very wet. The grinding is done carefully until all the wires are exposed and all glassy dips in the enamel have disappeared. Careful attention to the edges of the piece requires grinding a sloping edge that is evenly rounded.

I remove the dop stick by placing it in the freezer for a few minutes and letting the piece drop off in the warmth of my palm. Any wax residue is cleaned off with a knife. Holding the piece perpendicular to the sanding belt, remove any enamel from the edges. If you have an irregular edge, a large diamond bit in your Foredom hand piece will aid in this process. Remember to do all grinding wet. Next, the piece is vigorously cleaned with a glass brush under running water. Check that no speck of wax remains, as it will fire into the piece causing cloudiness and bubbles. I use clean, white, unscented paper towels to dry the work and then check that all the wires are exposed. If not, I regrind and glass brush. When the grinding is complete, the piece receives its final firing for a glossy and smooth surface.

If your wires extend to the edge of the piece, you may find a little lump at each wire edge, which could make a problem for burnishing a bezel smoothly over the edge of the enamel. I use my judgment at this point and often will return to the grinder, using a 15MIC sanding belt with about 600 grit, to refine the edge shape and then repeat the finishing steps and fire again.

A few tricks I have learned: *(**Note:** When I say layer, I mean apply and fire the coat of enamel.)*

- For a very light background, apply one to three thin layers in just the background, leaving the cells empty.

- For a dark background, I enamel everything but the background for one to three layers until the wirework is securely sealed to the base and then complete all the cells. The dark background can then be safely completed with several layers.

- To remove a speck, I carefully use a Foredom with a small diamond drill under water in a shallow bowl.

- I often use a design that has two long wires less than a millimeter apart. To prevent their being sucked together, tiny gold balls are placed between them in the first layer.

- To fill a cell with foil, I make a pattern by placing tracing paper over the embedded wires and do a gentle rubbing with the side of a pencil lead.

- For gold balls under the surface of the enamel, I wet pack a layer and push the balls into the enamel grains. Silver balls will sometimes cause stress cracks, as silver expands and contracts more than gold. To have gold balls on the surface, I complete the enameling and the grinding of the piece; then, using a diamond drill bit, I make depressions in the surface of the enamel for the balls, put them in place and re-fire to fuse them.

- If cracks appear in a finished piece made with Japanese leaded enamels on fine silver with 24k gold wires, the fault is probably with your counter enamel.

- Before the final firing in a larger piece, I warm my grandmother's antique iron on top of the kiln, fire the piece on mica, then quickly slide the piece and the mica onto a ceramic tile and gently weight it with the warm iron. It will hold its new shape for the final firing.

- To remove excess moisture before drying the enamel, I find that a folded square of unscented toilet paper that I pat gently over the enamel works well. I do not use the first few and the last few sheets of either the white Viva towels, which I prefer, or toilet paper because they have glue on them.

- To have a color deepen, I try to plan ahead so that I am adding colored transparents and not filling in with flux.

There is very much to be said for the merits of joyful experimentation and the fluidity of the creative process. There is no right or wrong way to approach this wonderful craft. I offer "my way" as a tool for you to find "your way."

Enameling On Electroformed Vessels
JUNE SCHWARCZ

Electroforming is electroplating when most of the surface has been thickened by plating. If you silver-plated a copper teapot, that would not be electroforming. Forming an object with thin copper foil and then thickening it with copper in a plating bath to make a sturdy vessel is electroforming. Most of my work is enameled with transparents, and my pieces vary in size from 3" to 11½". My method of working is governed by the form of the piece, as each piece is different. I am describing how I usually work. For more information on electroforming, see *Metal Techniques for Craftsmen* by Oppi Untracht.

Originally, I worked on sheet or spun copper pieces in the bàsse-taille technique over etched surfaces, to make shallow bowls or wall pieces. For bàsse-taille I apply transparent enamels that can be fired directly on copper without a coat of flux under them. I use the color as if I were making a watercolor painting, using different colors in each area, some thicker layers and some thinner. I apply leaded, soft flux to even out the coat of enamel and make the layer of enamel thick enough so that it will not burn out in the first firing. On the subsequent firings, I can use any color and continue to build up colors and flux according to aesthetic considerations.

In 1962, I became interested in electroplating. At first I was interested in electroplating in order to achieve greater depth for my etching of the bàsse-taille pieces. My husband, Leroy Schwarcz, who was a mechanical engineer, brought home a sample of thin copper foil that was about 1 mm thick. It proved to be good for making three-dimensional pieces. It had something of the quality of soft fabric but could be plated to be sturdy enough to handle and to enamel. I found I could make pleats with the foil and sew seams with thin copper wire to form the piece for electroforming.

My shapes are developed on newsprint that is then used as the pattern to cut the thin copper foil. It is important that the copper piece be absolutely clean when put into the tank to be plated and formed. I clean the copper with Sparex 2 and sometimes with sulfuric acid. Sometimes I coat the inside of the foil with melted wax before I put the formed piece in the bath. With the wax on the inside, the piece holds its shape as it is being electroplated. This wax must be completely removed after the plating is finished so that the copper can be enameled. The wax is melted and burned off. Then the piece is soaked in Sparex 2 again to remove the firescale, rinsed and wire brushed. Sometimes I use a sulfuric acid bath instead of the Sparex 2. It is then ready to be enameled.

I have a 30-gallon plating tank. It is about 17" high with the base 18" x 24". The formula I use for the bath is 28 to 30 oz. copper sulfate and 8 to 10 oz. concentrated sulfuric acid per gallon of water. I use a prepared copper sulfate solution although it is possible to make a bath of agricultural copper sulfate. Over time the amount of copper seems to increase in the solution. When this happens, some of this copper must be removed and more water and sulfuric acid added. I test the solution myself when I feel it needs testing. Experience with the results tells me when it needs to be strengthened.

My kiln is 15½"w x 18"h x 18"d on a 220V line. I fire at 1500°F. The number of times I fire varies a great deal depending on the design and aesthetic considerations. The number of firings also depends on whether the copper is beginning to blister. Blistering is my greatest problem in enameling electroformed pieces. If the blisters are very little under the enamel, I leave them. If they are large and break, showing black spots, then I clean them and re-enamel over them.

I usually sift on the enamels, but I sometimes wet-inlay the enamel instead if there is to be a pattern in my design. I use 80 mesh leaded enamels; some are Thompson's old ones and others are from various manufacturers. These enamels vary in their degree of fineness of grind. I use some of them just as they come, but if they are too powdery I sift away the fines, using Thompson's 200 and 300 mesh sifters.

The inside of a vessel is enameled first with medium or hard enamel. My husband made me some small sifters from slices of small medicine bottles and other rigid tubing that were attached to dowel sticks of varying lengths. I use them to sift the enamel onto the inside of vessels. I use an airbrush for spraying the 1:2 diluted Klyr-Fyre. I spray, sift, spray, sift, trying to have the Klyr-Fyre moisten all the particles. When the piece is dry, it is placed in the kiln with the bottom of the vessel toward the back of the kiln. A piece often requires an additional layer fired on the inside before the outside of the piece is enameled.

Occasionally I use a raku technique to get a luster effect. The colors change a little depending on the colors of the enamel used. To raku, I line the inside of a large canning pot with large Acanthus leaves. When the piece completes its final firing, I take it out of the kiln and quickly put the canning pot on top of it. You must leave it that way until it has cooled down somewhat. The piece must not cool off too quickly. You have to be making a fairly large enamel for this method to work. If you do not like the effect, you can fire it away in the kiln.

When I was first introduced to enameling by a student of Kenneth Bates, I was immediately interested in the transparent quality of enamels. Although I sometimes use a few opaques, my interest in the transparents has remained for forty-seven years while I have been working mostly on three-dimensional objects.

Large Cloisonné Wall Pieces on Copper
Marian Slepian

I have worked in cloisonné on large-scale wall hangings and site-specific installations for public spaces. My work ranges from 8" x 10" to several feet. I have also created a walk-in outdoor sculpture that has withstood time and the elements. Recently, I have been making fine silver cloisonné objects, but this article deals only with my large cloisonné enamels on copper.

I begin my work with a series of rough sketches on inexpensive newsprint I purchase by the bolt from a local newspaper. This paper is cheap, sturdy and large enough. I refine my sketches and then make a full size line drawing for the cloisonné wires. I do not color the drawings; I prefer to work the colors as I enamel.

My kiln is 18" x 18" x 12" on its own 220V line, so I have to make the enamel in sections no larger than 17". With this limitation in mind, I red line the drawing to indicate the cut lines for the metal. The cut pieces are my patterns for the 18 ga metal I cut with a metal shear and a nibbler. The nibbler cuts away a ¼" strip of scrap from the metal. Copper is wasted this way, but for very large pieces a lot of time is saved. The nibbler is what I call my electric shear that is used by roofers and metal workers. It is heavy, so it takes two of us to move it around. If the enamel is one piece with straight sides, I sometimes bend the sides in a flange. I also use a small nibbler (available from Micro-Mark, 340 Snyder Ave. Berkeley Heights, NJ 07922) and an electric Dremel saw for fine cutting pieces that fit on the saw's table. Any etching is done after all the pieces are cut.

My kiln was custom-built; it has a pyrometer and three sets of independently controlled elements. Firing is kept to 1450°F to prevent the fine-silver cloisonné wires from sinking into the copper and forming a eutectic, a metal alloy. The danger of this happening is increased by the size of the piece, so it is necessary to rotate the piece during the firing to distribute the heat more evenly. The areas closest to the elements will mature faster.

I use large amounts of silver cloisonné wire and, therefore, I can have it milled to my specifications. The wires that I order range from .005 to 16 ga, both round and flat.

The wire is priced by the ounce, and there is a 10-ounce minimum order of mixed sizes. I found that the 16 ga square wire could break loose in later firings.

Some pieces require more than 10 firings. Unlike silver on silver, silver on copper has an inherent danger, for the more the piece is fired, the greater the risk of a eutectic and also severe warping. Warping makes mounting nearly impossible. To reduce warping, when the piece comes out of the kiln, and is still white-hot, I sandwich it between two ¼" thick steel weights that are 18" square. I have developed muscles!

My leaded enamels are 80 mesh in the opaques and 100 mesh in the transparents. The back is counter enameled and a base coat of hard enamel is enameled on the front. These base coats are sifted. The drawing is transferred to the enamel with either carbon paper or fabric transfer paper, as both burn off cleanly. The wires are formed on the pencil drawing, bent with two jeweler's tweezers, cut, dipped in diluted Klyr-Fyre and set in place on the enameled base coat. Each piece is dusted with either opaque or transparent enamel after it has dried. It is then fired and cooled between the steel weights. The cloisonné wires do not distort from being weighted; they are pretty well anchored because I am careful to place them so that they touch the enamel. The very light dusting of enamel before the firing also helps to embed the wires in the enamel.

From this point on, all enameling is done by wet packing washed enamels. I use mostly opaques and then many layers of transparents for shading. Each subsequent firing requires strict attention to the kiln. A millisecond of too much heat can cause the sinking of some wires, which is a real problem to correct. You usually have to start that piece over again. For wet packing, I use a spatula to carry the wet enamels from their containers to the piece and a fine sable brush to pack them in place. I prefer multiple, thinly applied layers of enamel because I am ever cognizant of the possible eutectic; however, I do try to keep the number of firings as limited as possible. The entire piece is wet packed to the same level before each firing.

When the enameling is finished, I sometimes de-gloss the surface with an etch, but usually I leave it bright so that it will be seen better from a distance, which is how most of my work is viewed. To mount the finished piece or pieces, I use outdoor plywood, 3/8" thick, painted black and cut slightly smaller than the assembled enamel. The screws, flat-headed stove-bolts, are counter-sunk through the mounting board before the enamel is glued down. The wire for hanging is secured to these screws. The binders I use are a silicon material that is malleable but very reliable. My preference is the GE one, but I also use Dow or any other dependable brand name.

I prefer silicon to epoxy because the enamel piece can be sawn off with nylon fishing line if necessary.

Each piece is weighted with steel plates while the binder is drying. I have four different size weights of one or more inches thick with handles, plus some ¼" thick ones that are 12" x 15". I add an antique flat iron on top of these ¼" weights. The mounting depends on where the artwork is to be placed.

Layering Over Sgraffitoed Liquid Enamel Base Coat
JUDY STONE

I make light switch covers that are site-specific functional fine art and sculptural vessels that are not at all functional. I sgraffito my design into dried Thompson's #533 liquid white enamel base coat. I layer transparent, opaque and opalescent enamels over it in many firings. The white liquid enamel base coat over the metal is similar to a coat of gesso over canvas in oil painting. In subsequent firings, the layers go from transparent to opaque or dark to light.

I usually enamel on 18 ga copper. I form my switch cover shapes from copper sheet pressed in a hydraulic press with a masonite die. I either buy copper vessel shapes and alter them or I fabricate them from copper sheets. I like either to cut holes in the vessels or cut pieces out of them and then sew the pieces with copper wire or rivet copper pieces over the holes.

The copper is cleaned by firing the pieces in the kiln for about a minute at 1500°F. After the copper cools, I remove any loose firescale with a toothbrush. The base coats, front and back, are applied with an airbrush in the spray booth. I usually clean and spray several pieces at the same time. Thompson's #533 liquid white needs to be stirred until all lumps are dissolved and also diluted with water, if need be, to the right consistency for the airbrush. I prefer the even coating the airbrush can achieve. An uneven application usually results in a myriad of colors and textures. I spray only a small amount of the liquid enamel at a time because the heavier enamel particles tend to sink and must be agitated to keep them dispersed in solution. The airbrush needle is set way back in its tip, and the aperture is wide open to keep the heavy enamel material flowing evenly through the airbrush. When all pieces are coated, they are dried with a heat gun. Industrially, this is called "bisquing" because drying at 1200°F creates a very hard surface.

The hard surface of dried, white, liquid enamel is sgraffitoed with a sharpened bamboo skewer. The pieces become drawings, sometimes with very noticeable strokes, sometimes with different width lines or with large areas of exposed copper created by first scratching with the skewer and then brushing the enamel away with a soft brush.

If I am working on the three-dimensional vessel forms I will spray all sides with #533 and sgraffito all sides. If I am working on switch covers, I will brush a Thompson liquid counter enamel on the backs of the covers after sgraffitoing the fronts and then sift 80 and 100 mesh enamel over the still wet counter enamel.

The switch covers, with both sides coated for the first firing, are fired with the white side down on a point rack. The points are coated with kiln wash and allowed to dry before they are used. The vessels are fired concave side down on either a trivet or a fired support constructed for the piece. I fire to maturity at around 1500°F. The kiln I use is an old 220V Vcella with a fairly large chamber. It is very energy efficient and retains an even heat.

After the first firing, the pieces are put in a Sparex 2 bath to remove the firescale that has formed over the exposed copper lines and spaces, then rinsed well and dried. My procedure of layering has developed as my knowledge of enameling has grown and as I have learned about the three-dimensional aspects of the color I am working with. The first layer of enamel over my sgraffitoed surface is a sifting with a 150 mesh sifter of never more than four or five colors of Thompson's #150 mesh lead free transparents. I overlap some of the transparent enamels to suggest an under-painting that I will develop with subsequent layers. On the three-dimensional vessels, I airbrush diluted 1:4 Klyr-Fyre before sifting. The wetted particles must dry before I fire. This layer of sifted transparents is fired to orange peel at 1500°F. When they come out of the kiln, the switch covers are weighted with a press plate to minimize warping. The heat changes the vessel forms slightly during cooling, and I incorporate these changes while I create the piece.

The rest of the firings involve applying thin layers of wet enamel, gradually building toward the depth and color contrast I want. I am looking for very subtle colors with an opalescent quality that play against the first layer of transparents, which I have fired over white and over copper. The order of application before each firing is to apply wetted particles, dry the enamel, sift flux and fire. The enamels I use for wet application are 325 mesh Thompson lead free opaques, Japanese opalescents and a few miscellaneous enamels that have been spooned into watercolor palettes and a few drops of tap water added. With a brush, I push and pull the enamels, not wet packing, but using the water to guide the particles. I like to bring the particles as close to my sgraffitoed lines as possible. I tend to use the lines to form boundaries between various colors. I also like to mix enamels for subtle shading on a piece. After the wet particles have dried and before firing, I dust on a very thin layer of flux with a 150 mesh sifter. The flux I use is Blythe C-10 from England. It has a slightly yellow cast. The flux minimizes break up, especially from the lead free opaques. I slightly underfire though with the kiln at 1500°F. As the layers build, I may fire at a lower temperature or for a shorter time to control the amount of transparency I want as the underlayer of white becomes more transparent.

At various stages, I add glass elements such as balls, squares, slivers, threads and beads as accents and to give texture. I may also incorporate gold and silver foils in the later layers. The foils act as accents and also add to the imagery of the work. The foils I use are the thicker Japanese ones, some with a black overglaze pattern, and the thinner Thompson foils. I seldom cut foil pieces larger than one inch. The foil is placed in position with a wet brush and held in place with a drop of diluted Klyr-Fyre. Before firing, I sift a layer of Japanese silver flux (N-1 or S-302) with a 150 mesh sifter over the whole piece. The Japanese flux is softer than the Blythe flux. I continue to use the Japanese flux for any subsequent layers I might need once I have placed foil on a piece. I sometimes wet the piece to float some 60 mesh or coarser transparents over the fired foil and flux to give it color and then fire again.

I sign my name on the front of my pieces with Thompson's P-3, underglaze black, mixed with pine oil. When the signature is dry from being on top of the kiln, I sift on a thin layer of flux for the final firing. It takes from six to sixteen firings to complete one of my enamel pieces.

One option for finishing the enamel surface of a piece is satin finishing that I do for my vessel forms. I first file away any oxidation on the edges and then glass-etch the surface first with B&B etching solution and etching cream. This brand seems to be less toxic than others. I then use abrasive papers to arrive at the finish I want. I have a tub of water sitting by my finishing station. I dip the piece and the papers in the water and change the water as it gets cloudy from use. I start with 800 grit diamond cloth (a diamond impregnated rubber pad), then go to a silicon carbide paper. I progress from 1000 to 1200 to 1800 to 2000 grit silicon carbide papers. All the work is done by hand except for any nooks and crannies where I use 3M impregnated bristle discs on my flex shaft.

The pieces I choose to satin finish are the sculptural, "destructed" vessel forms that I call "Burnt Offering." These pieces reflect the conflicts I often feel in working with enamel. I view enamel as a rendering medium but when used on a three-dimensional form, the rendering must be in harmony with the structure and yet be more than decoration, pattern or design. These pieces must be precious and show the possibilities of ultimate control of the medium and at the same time must seem to be dissolving in chaos and destruction, never to be used to fulfill a function.

Jewelry Size Miniature Paintings
MONA SZABADOS

My enamel jewelry includes earrings, pins, pendants, lockets and rings done in Grisaille and Limoges techniques. Within most of the pieces are miniature paintings with images of women's faces and animals. My enamel pieces, using copper, 80 mesh enamels, ceramic pigments and foils, usually require from 25 to 40 firings. I collaborate with my husband, Alex, who is a goldsmith. Each enamel piece is set in 22K or 18K gold.

Usually I start my enamels by cutting out a copper shape and then do a rough sketch of the enamel for that piece. Sometimes I do the sketch first. Most often I have a very well defined color arrangement in mind, but it can change as I work.

I order 18 ga and 20 ga oxygen free, hardened copper (OFHC) in sheet form from American Copper & Brass in Oakland, CA. I use the Japanese 246 gold foil and pure silver foil from Thompson; I also use palladium leaf from Enamelwork Supply Co. The kiln I use the most is 9" x 8" x 6½" on a 110V line, but I also have a large kiln on a 220V line. Firing is at 1350-1400°F.

After the copper shape is cut, the metal is cleaned by firing at 1300°F for five minutes, then put into the pickle of 30% Sparex and 70% distilled water, rinsed and then glass brushed. I clean anywhere from one to six pieces at a time, depending on my work schedule. My enamels are the leaded, standard 80 mesh. I wash one to two teaspoons of a color with distilled water until the water is clear. The washed enamels are stored wet in fish and tackle containers in a closed wooden cabinet. They are re-rinsed with distilled water before I use them. I do not make color samples; I learn about the enamels as I use them.

Using 1/0 to 4/0 ¼" hair, sable brushes, I wet pack, with distilled water, medium or hard flux and transparent enamels on the front. Flux is wet packed over the face area and dark transparents over the other areas, without the flux and the dark transparents touching. This firing leaves a firescale line between the areas of the flux and the dark enamels. The enamel is packed about 1½ mm high, which after firing barely covers the copper. About four coats are applied on the front and fired before sifting dry enamel on the back. The enamel piece is supported on a trivet that is on a mesh planche for the firing. I brush off the loose firescale on the back of the piece between the firings and also clean the edge of the piece with a Carborundum stone. When there is an adequate base coat on the front, I sift counter enamel on the back over the remaining firescale. Any additional coats needed later on the back are wet packed.

Then I proceed with the firings on the front. Colorful transparents are added to the face for shadows and features. After each firing, the edge of the copper is rubbed with Carborundum stone to remove any firescale. For the face, I use Schauer's leaded opaque ivory color or white opalescent enamel, applying and firing about ten thin layers in the manner of grisaille, wet packing very wet and sculpting the enamel thicker on the forehead, the tip of the nose, etc. The thin areas of the opaque allow the transparent enamels to show through. Schauer is no longer manufacturing enamels, but fortunately I purchased a large supply. If I am planning to use silver foil in an area, then I use a cool color enamel under it.

To cut the foil, I place it between two sheets of typewriter paper. After separating the foil and the paper, I pick up a piece of foil with a brush that is wet with a 1:1 solution of Klyr-Fyre and distilled water and place it on the fired enamel. I used to always put silver flux over silver foil before applying a transparent pink or red, but now there are some leaded Japanese enamels that fire well without the flux under them. The transparent enamels generally will stay a lighter color if a coat of flux is fired between the layers.

In the last three firings, I very carefully use Thompson ceramic pigments in very small amounts (tiny dots) to strengthen the features of the face. Each color is mixed with distilled water in a section of a party ice cube tray; and then a small amount of each color is placed on an agate slate and mixed with a little imitation lavender oil. I use the imitation lavender oil because it dries faster. A box lid covers the slate palette to keep the pigments clean between working sessions. After two weeks of work, or when I do a show, the slate is cleaned off to be ready for a clean supply.

When the enameling is completed, I smooth the edges with a blue wheel on the flexible shaft. I set the enamel in the bezel Alex has made, and he sets any stones we have chosen for the piece we have designed together.

Risso Screen
Joann Tanzer

Traditional photo silk-screen was one of the techniques I taught as a Professor of Art at San Diego State University. The possibility of developing art images seemed endless, but the process of making screens was awkward and time consuming. To develop a library of silk-screen panels in the traditional way required space for storing and time for preparation.

When I attended a demonstration on silk-screening using Risso Screen, I was immediately struck with the potential of this process for enameling. The Japanese company that made the screen used it mainly to make greeting cards. I found it intriguing because there was an immediacy about it. One could make a screen in seconds. It did not require an involved preparation of the screen itself, a transparency for the use of the screen nor a bulky wooden frame.

With Risso screen (sometimes called speed screen or thermal screen), it became possible to develop a collection of eight to ten screens in minutes. I would like to make it understood that I did not invent this material, but rather found a use for it for enamels. Much of what has been done with Risso screen has been developed continually by students and artists in their studios.

What is Risso Screen? It is a green nylon mesh material that is both a screen and a film that is heat sensitive. It comes in rolls of various widths and several different meshes and also by the sheet. The roll comes with a plastic sheet in the package to support your carbon photo image and the screen through a thermal copier. By the sheet, instead of the plastic support sheet, the green screen comes with a piece of white paper attached to provide a sandwich to slide your photocopy into. You run the assemblage through the thermofax machine with everything facing up. On top is the rough side of the green mesh (the smooth underside etches your carbon photo copy into the screen), under the mesh sheet is your photo copy, right side up against the smooth side of the screen and under your copy sheet is either the plastic sheet or a piece of white paper as a support. A new thermal copier on the market is Vistafax. You may be able to find a second hand copy machine at a reasonable price. I have several machines. They range from a portable unit to one with a 24" opening. I even found one for $5 in a junkyard.

I usually buy the Risso screen in 70 or 100 mesh rolls. The image you make for your screen needs to be made with a photocopier because those machines make carbon copies. Welsh Products will sell single sheets of Risso. I advise beginners to start with the 70 mesh, which allows the 80 mesh enamel to pass through more easily than the 100 mesh screen does. The finer mesh gives a precise detail. The size screen you use depends on the opening in the thermal copier and the size of your kiln.

A screen allows the enamel artist another way of developing images, textures and patterns. Enamel falls onto prepared surfaces through the screen to make a precise image. The potential of this technique is unlimited. The use of the screen can be applied to any style or attitude of art. The technical information for screening can be as varied as the uses. I do not often use the screen as a single image, but as a series of small segments that together enrich the composition.

First, you need to make a graphite copy of what you want to screen. You can screen photographs, drawings, combinations of all kinds of markings, textures, patterns and collages. I like collages because they are so serendipitous. Dissected news photographs are a wonderful place to start. I cut out quantities of material from newspapers, magazines and even cereal boxes. Anything is fair game. When I am ready to make aesthetic judgments of my collection of visual images, I arrange the clippings on a stiff paper surface. Once I have chosen the image, I photocopy it. This creates a graphite image that will become the pattern of the actual screen. Any copier that uses graphite can be used. You can use any technique, e.g., pencil, ink, photos, to make your image for a graphite copy. **Note:** the copy image cannot have large areas of black because black will stick to the screen. If you want to use a black image, run it through the machine several times to lighten the area and result in a satisfactory screen.

The Risso screen needs to be in a frame to hold it taut for the enamel to be worked through it. The frame can be purchased in plastic or cardboard. The frame will hold the screen about 1/16" above the metal or enameled tile so as not to disturb the enamel when the screen is removed. When I make a frame, I usually attach a lifter to the frame to help. The lifter is a spacer made of bits of very thin cardboard or other material. I like to make my frame with a 14" embroidery hoop. To use an embroidery hoop, take the finished screen and center it on an 18" square piece of cotton fabric or rip cloth, which dries very fast if it gets wet. Sew the material onto the screen around the edge, leaving enough material to stretch the cloth taut into the hoop. Then cut out the section of material under the screen. Screens do not need to be stored in their frames. You will be able to save and keep many screens in a small area such as a loose-leaf binder with plastic sleeves. The screens can be folded for storage.

The Risso screen sheet, about 9" x 11½", looks like a sheet of shiny green paper that is attached at the short ends to a piece of white paper and is open on the two long sides. To make a Risso screen, place your photocopied image face up in the open pocket with the green side up. With a small piece of Risso screen make a test run with an image that fits the scrap. The "sandwich" is run through the Thermofax machine with the green side (the shiny side) up. The proper setting on the 3M Thermofax varies with each machine. Start with #5 on the dial. Move the setting up or down until you get a clear image.

Feed your blank paper, image and screen into the thermal machine at the proper setting. It will automatically return to you. I usually run them through two or three times to check for clarity and a strong, crisp image. I check the screen by folding back one corner and holding it up to the light. If the screen is cut properly, you will see a sharp imprint of your image. Stretch the screen in a taut manner to a frame. The screen may be used on bare metal that accepts enamel or on a flat piece of pre-enameled copper, fine silver or steel. Before you work on a large piece, I suggest you make some samples on either 2" or 4" square tiles. I assume that you know about various metals, enamels and firing. For base coats, I use medium or hard, light color opaques or hard flux.

For dry screening, I use 80 mesh, unwashed, medium fusing enamels and sometimes soft enamels for the final coat. I place the screen in a Welsh Products plastic, adjustable frame, which I use raised up 1/16" high so that the enamel will not be disturbed when the screen is removed. You can use either a stiff 3" x 5" card, a plastic credit card or a commercial squeegee to push the enamel through the screen onto the flat metal or enameled surface. Lift the screen off carefully and place the piece onto stilts or whatever you use to support the piece in the kiln. Fire at 1500°F until the enamel is fused, remove the piece from the kiln and weight the enamel piece if necessary.

To use a wet enamel, I prefer using the screen sewed to fabric and stretched in the embroidery hoop. The plastic frame is satisfactory also. I use dry crackle color that I mix with water to the consistency of cold cream. I push the enamel through the screen with a rubber or plastic cot on my forefinger or you can use a tool. The wet enamel gives you great control, and the colors can be quickly changed or mixed on the screen. If you wash the screen very soon after using, it will stay in better condition. The washing does not injure the screen, but do it gently.

The screen may be allowed to dry, dried in the sun or with a hair dryer. Many layers of the wet surface can be applied before firing, but allow a drying period between coats of the screened image. Much editing can occur when the enamel has dried on the panel. You can sgraffito or remove areas with a brush, stick or card.

Here are some suggestions on ways to use the screen on 2" x 2" copper samples:

1. Apply opaque enamel >> fire >> screen opaque image in contrasting color.

2. Apply light opaque enamel >> fire >> screen dark transparent color.

3. Apply flux >> fire >> screen opaque dark color.

4. Apply light transparent color >> fire >> screen dark transparent color.

5. Screen transparent image on raw copper >> fire >> fire a light transparent.

6. Then try all of the above in multiples of overlays. Using a single screen image, juxtapose the image over and over, still retaining the feeling of the original. Explore with color themes and relationships to achieve desired results.

The possibilities are only limited by your imagination and your knowledge of how the various enamels fire. As you accumulate a collection of screens you will find their versatility endless.

Cloisonné On Steel
Joseph Trippetti

Design is my main interest. My method of enameling has remained about the same these many years. Originally, my work was mainly of cloisonné on domed copper plaques. I trained as a metalsmith. For the past 15 years I have been working on white pre-coated, flanged, steel plaques, ranging in size from 6" x 6" to 16" x 20". Using the pre-coated, steel tiles I do not have to be concerned with cleaning the metal and applying base coats. The fine silver, rectangular cloisonné wire I use is .010 x .035.

I have two Norman kilns, 15" x 15" x 9" and 27" x 24" x 15", on a 220V line. They were made for me with the specification to heat within 35 minutes and have fast recovery. Each kiln has a pyrometer, and I fire between 1250°F and 1500°F. My pyrometer has not been checked for years, and so my kiln temperature may be way off a standard, but it works for me. The floor of the kiln is protected with a Fiberfax blanket. Firebricks support the flanged piece in the kiln. I do use a timer, especially for the larger pieces, to remind me to look in the kiln after 3½ to 4 minutes, at which time the piece is usually about orange peel stage. This method is adequate for all except the final firing. I usually eyeball it. Originally the kiln wires were exposed, but when a pitting problem developed, the wires were changed to be covered in the floor of the kiln.

I start with rough sketches in pencil and then translate the selected one to a full size ink drawing. Using carbon paper, like dressmaker carbon paper that leaves no residue, the pen drawing is transferred to the pre-coated steel plaque. To protect the drawing, I tape a sheet of glass to foam board and make a sandwich into which I slip the drawing. The pen drawing is used as a pattern to bend the cloisonné wires. I form the wires on top of the glass and then position each wire on the transferred design on the plaque.

The tool for bending the wires is one I designed by soldering a handle of the tweezers to one of the handles of a straight bezel shears. The tweezers and my fingers are used to bend the wire; the short blades of the bezel shears cut the wire in place on the glass. My aim is to take the least complicated approach. The cloisonné wires are put in place on the plaque with uncut Klyr-Fyre. After the Klyr-Fyre has dried, the piece is fired. With my kiln at 1300°F, a 16" x 16" plaque is placed in the kiln and the timer set for 3½ to 4 minutes. Subsequent firings are at around 1300°F to avoid overfiring the piece. Through all the firings, as with silver cloisonné wires on copper, overfiring can cause the wires to sink into the enamel.

I use primarily 80 mesh opaque, leaded, unwashed enamels, though I also have some 150 mesh enamels and some unleaded enamels that I use when I need those colors. To use them all in one piece, the unleaded enamel needs to be under the leaded enamel and not on top. The enamels, wet with water, are wet packed with a brush almost to the top of the wires, and then the piece is tapped to level out the enamel and fired. Before each firing, any opaque enamel on the wires is removed with a fine pointed brush. It usually takes about 8 to 10 applications of the enamel, tapping and firing for the fired enamel to reach almost the top of the wires.

The final firing, with just a thin sifting of either soft or medium flux over the whole piece, is a healthy firing with the kiln at 1500°F before inserting the plaque into the kiln. I do not wet the piece for the sifted coat. My sifters are made of 80 mesh screen bent into open boxes in square or rectangular shapes. The square ones are about 2½" x ½" deep. I also have ones that I soft soldered together out of brass tubing.

I do not remove the veil of flux from the wires after the final firing. This coating protects the fine silver wires from discoloring. You need to be careful not to overfire this final firing in order to prevent the flux on the wires from balling up. For me, the most important stage in the making of each enamel is the pen drawing of my design.

Enameling on Fine Silver Metal Clay
Jean Vormelker

Enameling on pieces made from Precious Metal Clay is a joy! The clay is malleable and will take any shape or texture: it handles like ordinary clay before it is sintered. After the sintering, the material is usable in a variety of enameling techniques. Sintering, an evaporation process, is done by firing the formed clay in a kiln at a high temperature that removes the binder and water and compresses the minute metal particles into solid metal. After sintering, the object is pure silver or gold and is enameled as such.

Metal clay has the possibility for unusual shapes. There is no waste: all scrap is reusable one way or another. Pieces can be prepared for champlevé without etching or soldering. The ultimate joy from metal clay is that there is no copper to oxidize and cause firescale problems.

The metal clay brands that I have worked with are Precious Metal Clay (PMC), made by Mitsubishi Materials Corp. and Art Clay, made by Aida Chemical Corp. Original PMC is a less sticky formulation than PMC+ and Art Clay. They all look like window putty and are worked like ceramic clay. Both brands are available in different formulations: lump form, paste, slip/syringe and paper/sheet. The new PMC Paper is very flexible and can be folded like Origami. Unlike the other forms, it only sticks to itself when water is applied to it. This is a growing field with exciting new formulations added periodically. Given a choice, my students usually prefer to use PMC+ because there is less shrinkage and shorter sintering time.

For earrings, pins, pendants, necklaces and other light stress or larger objects, my choice is the original PMC formulation. The pieces are relatively lightweight compared to fabricated forms of the same metals. The shrinkage of 25-30% allows detail that could not be done any other way. It is the most porous formulation. For rings or bracelets, PMC+ or Art Clay Silver with 10-12% shrinkage are better choices because the metal is denser and will better withstand abuse.

You can buy the metal clay in either fine silver (.999), fine gold (24K PMC) or 22K Art Clay gold. The paste and slip formulations are useful in making multi-part pieces and decoration. PMC is sold by the Troy ounce, 31.1 grams of silver plus binder and water. One ounce of PMC is about the size of the end joint of a woman's thumb.

PMC+ and Art Clay have more silver, less binder and water per ounce, so an ounce of these is smaller in size and sold by the avoirdupois ounce, 28.35 grams.

Producing a silver or gold object with metal clay is adequately covered in today's literature, so I am covering mainly my method of enameling on silver after I have made the piece. Sometimes I sketch an idea, but I rarely draw a design in detail. Part of my inspiration comes from working intuitively and directly with the material.

The most important decision to be made after sintering is how to finish the surface of the piece before enameling. I can choose to leave areas the natural matte white of sintered silver, brass brush it to a satin finish or burnish it to a high polish. I like the look of just burnishing the raised surfaces. A variety of finishes adds a visual depth to the piece as well.

Transparent enamels reflect slightly different shades of the same color depending on the surface finish of the silver below it and, therefore, how the light reflects from it. The color will differ, e.g., between the valleys with a matte or satin finish and the highly polished ridges. If a variation of color is desired, the valleys can remain a matte or satin finish and the ridges can be highly polished. However, to have a consistent color regardless of how the light hits it, the surface must be finished evenly whether it is matte, satin or burnished. This finishing is particularly important on smooth surfaces where every flaw is noticeable.

Bring up the shine gradually, stopping to evaluate at each step. It is hard to go back to the original softer finish if the whole piece is burnished to a hard bright shine in the beginning. Taking care not to disturb the areas I want to remain matte white, I usually start with a brass brushed satin finish to bring up the metallic color on the parts to be shined. Then the burnishing closes the pores of the silver and puts on a high shine. If the surface of the metal is not closed by burnishing, excess air bubbles might form in the enamel because of porosity in the metal. My PMC test pieces showed that using the tumbler for an all-over burnished surface produces fewer small air bubbles in the enamel than hand-burnishing. Enameling requires a clean surface, so I do not use a buffing machine, which might leave polishing compounds that could be difficult to remove. An overall high shine is best done in a tumbler with steel shot, a little Fels Naptha soap and water.

I have used 80 mesh, unwashed, leaded and unleaded enamels in thin coats without discernable loss of brilliance. Counter enamel has not been necessary on thicker pieces when thin coats of enamel are used. I apply the enamel by wet packing or sifting. I only use an adhesive when the shape requires one. I have a Vcella enameling kiln, 12" x 12" x 6½", on a 220V line, and a SC-2 Paragon 8" x 8" x 6" controlled kiln for PMC on a 110V line.

Enamel colors appear different over silver than over copper. I made separate color charts of leaded and unleaded transparent enamels on PMC using both sides of the piece. For the leaded enamels, I made a piece of PMC, finished size 1½" x 3" x 22 ga, with a tumble burnished finish. Unwashed dry enamel colors are applied in ¼" blocks over alternating ¼" stripes of bare silver and a base coat of Ninomiya N-1 Flux for Silver. This color chart tells me which colors need the flux under them. Some colors do not look good either way; others look fine with or without the flux. I love Ninomiya N-1 Flux for silver. Other fluxes for silver I have used turned yellow, but N-1 stays crystal clear.

My unleaded color charts are on two smaller pieces of PMC, with one side showing the colors over flux and the other side showing them on bare silver. I can view the whole spectrum for the same base or flip to the other side to see the same colors over both silver and flux.

Applying enamel to sintered and polished PMC or Art Clay pieces is the same as enameling on any other fabricated or cast metal. You can sift or wet pack 80 mesh enamel as usual. Firing temperature should be kept low, 1335°F-1400°F. Higher temperatures may change the color and may put an unpredictable metallic sheen on some enamels.

I continue to experiment with metal clay. An interesting variation is to apply dry enamel to the unfired dry clay piece before sintering. The piece can be left with the matte surface or the clay burnished before applying the enamel. I recommend using either the PMC+ or Art Clay for this technique. If PMC+ is used and sintered at the lower 1470°F for a half hour, enamel will stay on the surface and leave a clear silver back surface. The finished sample I have made with regular PMC using dry enamel before sintering has a lovely matte enamel surface. The drawback with this technique is that the enamel will sink all the way through the piece during sintering because of the greater porosity of PMC and leave a stained, blotchy look on the back, at best. Use this technique with PMC only on pieces where the back will be covered or enclosed. My sample did not show the darker colors usually associated with long, hot sintering.

If you plan to fire the enamel longer than the usual two minutes at 1335°F-1400°F, it would be wise to make a color chart using the longer sintering time and temperature for this technique. Look at your first color chart to choose appropriate colors to test. Avoid reds and oranges as they darken quickly.

Another technique that I have been experimenting with is the making of a new glass/metal alloy. I roll a small quantity of PMC+ in some enamel or add a small quantity of enamel, no more than 10-20%, to the clay, and thoroughly mix in the enamel. Remember the clay shrinks when fired, and if too much enamel is used, it will be squeezed out in unpredictable ways. Put a pattern on the piece and let it dry on a kiln shelf coated with kiln wash to prevent the enamel from sticking to the shelf. Fire at 1470°F for a half hour to sinter. Depending on how much enamel is used and how well mixed it is with the clay, the piece has anywhere from a shiny enamel surface to a grainy satin finish with glass throughout the piece.

In my samples of this alloy technique, I used Thompson's lead free transparent #2530 Water. Fired normally on the finished metal, it gave a lovely medium blue where applied thickly and a pale blue where thin. The same enamel when mixed with PMC+ and sintered for a half hour at 1470°F retained its light blue color as the silver turned to a matte white color. As the temperature was increased for the finished metal piece to 1560°F-1650°F for 20 minutes, and 10 minutes for the enamel, the color turned a darker olive green. Only color tests could have shown me what color change to expect.

Color samples are invaluable. In my very first enamel alloy experiment, I used PMC and Thompson's leaded #715-Blue Jay, mixing about 50% to 50% by volume. The pieces were fired at 1650°F for two hours. Alumina hydrate, a very finely granulated powder used to support pieces like beads that you do not want to flatten out in sintering, supported the pieces and kept the enamel off the kiln shelf. The pieces fired to an uneven, very dark — almost black — color on the front with huge lumps of dark enamel that were squeezed out on the back. Where the enamel touched the alumina, there was a matte gray grainy surface. This result was not a pretty sight, but it was a wonderful teaching tool.

One of the unique qualities of metal clay that I particularly like is its ability to make a seamless blending of different karats of gold. Ropes, rolls or worms of 18K and 24K gold PMC placed side by side and rolled together create a sheet of blended colors that is impossible to duplicate any other way. Although fine metals are too soft for some pieces, metal clays with their unique properties are a wonderful addition to the lexicon of metal techniques for the enamelist.

Liquid Flux as Etching Resist Bàsse-Taille

Phyllis Wallen

Editor's note: Phyllis described her technique for me more than twenty years ago. Phyllis died September 28, 2000. Her method of working is still current, and I am glad to be able to include it in this book. The liquid flux that Phyllis used as her etching resist was similar to the opalescent crackle Doris Hall used that predated the liquid flux.

In bàsse-taille (bahs ty), the metal has a design or a texture partially cut into its surface before being completely covered with transparent enamels, which allows the design or texture to be seen. Engraving and etching are among the many methods for cutting the metal. A resist is first painted on the areas that are not to be etched before the metal piece is placed in an acid bath. Among the materials that can be used for the resist are Klyr-Koat liquid flux, Thompson's medium fusing liquid flux and crackle. This description uses the Klyr-Koat liquid flux as the resist and nitric acid for the etching bath. After coating the metal with the liquid flux, the dried coat is sgraffitoed to expose the metal that will be etched. After the sgraffitoing the liquid flux coat is fired. This fired coat of enamel is the resist for the etching.

The liquid flux is applied by dipping a cleaned 18 ga copper plate or bowl in a shallow bowl with the liquid flux. The liquid flux is first tested with a spoon to determine whether it is the right consistency. You can tell by the way it coats the spoon. If the flux is too thick, distilled water is added one drop at a time. If it is too thin, then it has to be set aside until some of the water evaporates. Some of the binder will be lost if you spill out the excess water. The material needs to be stirred often while it is being used because it settles to the bottom of the container. With experience you will learn the right thickness for this base coat. If it is too thick, then when it dries you will not be able to draw any fine lines in it.

After you dip the copper piece in the liquid flux, shake off the excess into the container and place the piece upside down on a hammock or trivet until the coating on the front and the back dries. The dry, unfired liquid flux is very sensitive and will show every touch or water mark. If you make a mistake in your drawing, remove all of it and dip the piece again. Patches will show when the piece is fired. The design or texture to be etched is sgraffitoed with any kind of a pointed tool; the finer the point, the thinner the etched line will be.

To prevent the dry liquid flux on the back of the piece from rubbing off while you draw on the front, place the piece on a slick surface, e.g., a piece of plastic or a shiny magazine cover. There will often be a thick accumulation of dried liquid flux around the face edge of the piece. This edge should be shaved down gently and gradually to almost the same thickness as the rest of the coat. You can use a ¼" dia dowel piece to thin down the dried liquid flux or any smooth tool. When the drawing is completed, the loose dry flux is tapped off and the piece is fired to maturity in the kiln at 1500°F. You will see your drawing in an oxidized line or pattern on the front and a layer of fired flux on the back when the piece is removed from the kiln. If there are any unwanted small pit marks in the flux, cover them with clear lacquer nail polish before placing the piece in the acid bath.

Make an etching bath solution of one part nitric acid to three parts water. **Never pour water into the acid; always pour acid into the water to dilute the acid.** Pour the water into a photographer's rubber tray and then gently pour in the nitric acid. You can also put the bath in a Pyrex container and then place it on an electric warming tray set on low. The nitric solution etches faster when it is warm, but do not let the solution get hot or it will melt any lacquer or cause the enamel to move. A 6" copper plate will etch in from 30 minutes to one hour. On a cold day in a cool solution, the etching can take two to three hours. Most writers say you get better etch with a slower etch, but Phyllis said she got a better line with a faster etch.

The depth of the cut in the metal, called the "bite" in etching, should be limited to one-third to one-half the thickness of the metal. Most enamelists use 14 ga to 16 ga for a deep bite and 18 ga for a shallow bite. Phyllis used 18 ga for her bàsse-taille plates and bowls.

When the etching process is complete, the piece is rinsed thoroughly, scrubbed with a brush under running water, and then dried. The oxidized lines are burnished with a glass fiber brush to brighten the copper so that they will be a golden flux color. For the first application of transparent, 80 mesh, leaded enamel, either Thompson's #333 hard flux or #728 Amber is used. The enamel has been washed and dried. It is sifted on dry and pressed into the etched areas. Care must be taken to pack the enamel well along the ridges of the etched lines.

If this first fired coat of the 80 mesh does not cover completely, the piece again is placed in the acid solution to remove the firescale and is rinsed well before another coat of that same transparent enamel is applied and fired. If the edge of the piece is ragged from being eaten away in the acid solution, it is ground or filed smooth at this point. Color transparents are applied and fired in thin layers; the firescale is removed from the edge of the piece between firings.

Generally, each coat is fired to maturity. The counter enamel is applied immediately after the first transparent firing on the front. If there are blemishes on the back, then the counter enamel needs to be a mixture of transparents and opaques to cover them. The counter enamel usually needs an additional coat as a last firing for the piece. Thick coats of transparent color may produce a cloudy final coat instead of the clear, brilliant transparent enamel that is desired. Make the last firing as fast and as high as you dare in order to add brilliancy to the transparent enamels. The edge of the piece is filed and then polished to a smooth finish to complete it.

Cloisonné Opaque Enamel Jewelry
Ginny Whitney

I make brooches and pendants in abstract designs. For cloisonné pieces I use either fine silver, 24K gold or milled binding wires. When the enameling is completed, the piece is hand stoned to a matte, smooth surface. I rarely do multiples. My kiln is a medium size, conventional electric one.

A piece starts with a rough idea of size and colors and then proceeds to detailed working drawings which show colors, cloisonné wires if used, shape of piece and sometimes placement of pin findings or location of cable if applicable. My work ranges from ½" to 7". I keep careful color notes of my work for reference instead of making enamel color samples.

The metals used for the enameling are either copper or fine silver, sawed out from a 24 ga sheet. The metal is cleaned with pumice, followed by a final wipe with denatured alcohol solvent, then rinsed and dried. I use leaded Thompson and Schauer 80 mesh vitreous enamels in hard, medium and soft fusing. Frequently, I mix several colors together to get the desired color. Each enamel is washed with tap water in the traditional method. I fill the working container with about a tablespoon of enamel, add a lot of water, stir and let the enamel settle, pour off the cloudy water and repeat until the water is clear. I wet pack the wet enamels with a fine brush.

The cloisonné wires of binding wire are made by milling down various gauges until I get the size line I want. This cloisonné wire provides the line that separates the colors. For the fine silver or gold cloisonné wire, I cut a narrow ribbon off a piece of bezel or sheet and proceed as above. I use the binding wire cloisons when I want a black line without any intricate curves because it is not as soft as the fine silver and fine gold.

My pieces are counter enameled with medium flux that is wet packed on the back, dried with tissue and then turned over onto a piece of mica. Cloisonné wires are placed on the top surface, and the wet opaque enamels are applied with a small brush or fine metal spatula. When the first application is complete, the piece, with underlying mica, is carefully placed on a stainless grid and dried slowly under an electric light. The drying can take from 15 to 20 minutes. The whole unit — enamel, mica and grid — goes into a preheated 1500°F kiln. I fire between 1450°F and 1500°F. When the enamel is fused, the unit is removed and allowed to cool. Another layer of enamel is applied and fired. Then third and fourth applications are made to the front and flux is reapplied to the underside if needed.

The mica is pulled off the back when the enameling is completed and the piece is cool. The piece is stoned with a wet Carborundum stone to even the surface, change the shiny, glassy surface to matte and produce a smooth surface. Another task of the stoning process is to slope the edge evenly like a cabochon.

I construct a bezel setting with fine silver and sterling or with 24K and 18K gold with the appropriate findings for the brooch or pendant.

CHARTS

Approximate Color - Temperature Inside Kiln

Dull red	650°C	1200°F
Warm red	750°C	1380°F
Cherry	800°C	1470°F
Bright red	900°C	1650°F
White	1280°C	2330°F

Ceramic Firing Cones

016	735°C	1357°F
015	770°C	1418°F
014	795°C	1463°F
013	825°C	1517°F

Metal Melting Point

Copper	1083°C	1980°F
Gold	1060°C	1945°F
Fine Silver	960°C	1760°F
Sterling	898°C	1640°F
Steel	1350°C	2460°F

Silver Solder

	Melting Point	Flow Point
IT	1340°F	1490°F
Hard		1425°F
Medium	1335°F	1390°F

Metal Gauges and Weights

B & S	Inches	Millimeters	Drill Bit	Copper lb. Wt. sq. ft.	Sterling Silver sq. in. Troy oz.
28 ga	.012	.305	80		
26	.015	.381	79	.71	.087
24	.020	.508	76	.89	.110
22	.025	.635	72	1.13	.139
20	.032	.813	67	1.41	.175
18	.040	1.016	59/60	1.79	.221
16	.050	1.270	55/56	2.25	.278
14	.064	1.625	52	3.84	.351

Avoirdupois Weight

28.35 gm = 1 ounce
16 drams = 1 ounce
16 oz. = 1 pound

Troy Weight

24 grains = 1 dwt.
20 pennyweights (dwt) = 1 ounce
12 ounces = 1 pound

Gram Weight

31.103 gm. = 1 troy oz.
1.555 gm. = 1 troy dwt.

GUILDS AND SOCIETIES
Courtesy of *Glass on Metal*

National Enamelist Guild (est. 1973)
Kathy Bransford, President
1802 Brookstone Court
Vienna, VA 22182

Enamel Guild South, Inc. (est. 1975)
Eileen Gately, President
19601 N.E. 24th Avenue
N. Miami Beach, FL 33180
E-mail: egately@miami.med.edu
Audrey B. Komrad, Newsletter Editor
5720 Maggiore Street
Coral Gables, FL 33146

Palm Beach Enamel Guild
Margery Prilik, President
89 Seville 'F'
Delray Beach, FL 33446
Phone (561) 638-3477
A.R. Levine, Communications Contact
867 Lakeside Drive
North Palm Beach, FL 33408

Enamel Guild: West
Steve Artz, President
Jean Vormelker, Editor, *Vitreous Voice*
425 N. Shattuck Place
Orange, CA 92866-1232
E-mail: jean@jvormelker.com

San Diego Enamel Guild (est. 1981)
James Mayfield, President
E-mail: lawman007@juno.com
Studio 5 - Spanish Village Art Center
Balboa Park, CA 92101

Northern California Enamel Guild (est. 1975)
Stephanie Kaehler, President
Sandra E. Bradshaw, Newsletter Editor
Judy Stone, Corresponding Secretary
P.O. Box 254
El Cerrito, CA 94530
E-mail: jstone@cwnet.com

Cloisonné Collectors Club (1974)
Kay Whitcomb, Editor & V. President
109 South Street
Rockport, MA 01966

Northwest Enamelist Guild
c/o Ely E. Wilder, President
892 10th Court
La Fayette, OR 97127
Phone (503) 864-2403

Enamel Guild of New Jersey
Marian Slepian
5 Overlook Drive
Bridgewater, NJ 08807

Ohio Valley Enameling Guild
P.O. Box 310
Newport, KY 41072
Phone (859) 291-3800

Enamel Guild of Creative Arts Group
108 N. Baldwin Avenue
Sierra Madre, CA 91024

Enamel Guild/North East
Sandra Kravitz, President
115 Willow Street
Roslyn, NY 11577
Phone (516) 621-5584
E-mail: Alexandra_k@homemail.com
Lois Grebe, Secretary
7 Beechwood Road
Verona, NJ 07044
Phone (973) 239-9042
E-mail: Grebe@home.com

Australian Enamel Newsletter
c/o B. Ryman
71 George Street
Thirroul 2515
NSW Australia

eNAMEL Online Newsletter
Allan Heywood, Editor
http://users.netconnect.com.au/~enews/

The Enamellers Association
c/o Mrs. Heidi Wellings
15 Dewrang Avenue
Elanora Heights, 2101
Sydney, Australia

Japan Enamelling Artist Association
6F-A Asakawa Bldg. 1-19-13
Hyakunin-cho, Shinjyuku-ku
Tokyo, Japan, 169
Phone 03-367-3587

Japan Shippo Conference
Yohko Yoshimura
Kanda-Nishikicho Bldg. 403
3-20 Kanda-Nishikicho
Chiyoda-Ku Tokyo, Japan
Phone/FAX 03-3219-7805

Society of Dutch Enamellers (est. 1983)
http://www.enamellers.nl
Gré Dubbeldam, President
De Galop 15, 8252 Dronten, the Netherlands
Phone/FAX +31-321-313.661
E-mail: voorzitter@enamellers.nl
Tine Hardeman, Secretary
Vollenhoveschans 3, 1324 HS Almere-Stad,
The Netherlands
Phone/FAX +31-36-533.57.22
E-mail: secretaris@enamellers.nl

Society of British Enamellers
Ian Robertson, Chairman
Pat Johnson, Newsletter Editor
51 Webbs Road
London SW11 6RX England
E-mail: pat.johnson@enamel.demon.co.uk

The Guild of Enamellers
Geoffrey Winter, Publicity Officer
Brighton Road, Lower Kingswood
Tadworth, Surrey KT20 6SX England
Phone 01737 830082

Creativ-Kreis International - Italy
Mrs. Miranda Rognoni, President
Via Kennedy, 4
20048 Carate Brianza
Milan, Italy
Phone/FAX 0362-905972

The Canadian Enamellist Association
David Hustler, President
1 Ojibway Avenue
Toronto, Ontario, M5J 2C9 Canada
Phone (416) 203-0962

Pacific Canada Enamelists
8443 Hudson Street
Vancouver, B.C. V6P 4M3 Canada

Enamel Section, Israel Designer
Craftsmen's Association
Marga Michaeli, Coordinator
P.O. Box 17087
Tel Aviv 61170
Israel
Centre D' Informacio I Difusio
De L'Art De L'Esmalt
citutat de balaguer, 17 Llotja
Barcelona 08022
Spain

Kunstverein Coburg E.V.
Kurt Neun
Hans-Holbein-Weg 10
D-96450 Coburg
Germany

Creativ-Kreis International
Gertrud Rittmann-Fischer
D-54534 Grosslittgen
Himmerod 4
Germany

Asociacion Mexicana de Esmaltistas A.C. (est. 1991)
(Association of Mexican Enamelists)
Lilia Quintero H., President
Retorno Alajuela Num. 3.
San Jeronimo Lidice
Mexico 10200 D.F.
FAX (52) 55.95.20.03

Hungarian Enamel Center (est. 1975)
Nemzetközi Zománcmüvészeti
Alkotómühely (Turi Endre, Director)
Bethlen krt. 16
H-6000 Kecskemét,
Hungary

GIRAEFE
Marie-Thérèse Masias, President
2, Chemin du Tir
F-3940 Morez, France

Russian Center International
RCJ "Emalis"
Alexandr Karikh
Ulitsa Swobody, House 56, Whg. 38
Jaroslawl 150014
Russia

The India Enamel Society
c/o Veenu Shah
B-25, Chiragh Enclave
New Delhi - 110048 India
E-mail: VeenuS@nde.vsnl.net.in

SUPPLIERS

Copper
Passaic Metal & Building Supplies, Inc., 5 Central Ave., Clifton, NJ 07015-1849, Fax (973) 546-7179
Metalliferous, 34 West 46th St., New York, NY 10036 (212) 944-0909
American Metalcraft, 2074 George St., Melrose Park, IL 60160-1515, (800) 333-9133
American Copper & Brass, Oakland, CA

Refiners
Hoover & Strong, Inc., Richmond, VA, (800) 759-9997
Hauser & Miller Co., 10950 Lin-Valle Dr., St. Louis, MO 63123, (800) 462-7447
Handy & Harman Co., 525 Nuber Ave., Mt. Vernon, NY 10550 (gold)

Jewelry Tools, Metals and Findings
Myron Tobak, 25 West 47th St., New York, NY 10036, (800) 223-7550
W. R. Cobb Company, 850 Wellington Ave., Cranston, RI 02910, (800) 428-0040
Frei & Borel, P.O. Box 796, 126 Second St., Oakland, CA 94604, (800) 772-3456
Rio Grande, 6901 Washington NE, Albuquerque, NM 87109, (800) 545-6566
    www.riogrande.com
Indian Jewelers Supply Co., 601 East Coal Ave., Gallup, NM 87301, (505) 722-4451
Joseph P. Stachura Company, Inc., 435 Quaker Highway, Uxbridge, MA 01569, (508) 278-6525
T.B. Hagstog & Son, 709 Sansom St., Philadelphia, PA 19106, (800) 922-1006
Allcraft, 135 West 29th St., Suite 402, New York, NY 10001, (800) 645-7124
Salvadore Tool & Findings, Inc., 24 Althea Street, Providence, RI 02907, (401) 272-4100
SNAG (Society of North American Goldsmiths) publication, *Metalsmith*

Enamels, etc.
Thompson Enamel Inc., PO Box 310, Newport, KY 41072, (800) 545-2776
Bovano of Chesire, 800 South Main Cheshire, CT, (800) 847-3192
    (Soyer French Enamels)

Japanese Ninomaya Enamels
Enamelwork Supply Co., 1022 N.E. 68th St., Seattle, WA 98115, (800) 596-3247
The Enamel Emporium, 1221 Campbell Road, Houston, TX 77055, (713) 984-0552
Leslie Ceramics, 1212 San Pablo Ave., Berkeley, CA 94706, (510) 524-7363
Schlaifer's Enameling Supplies, 1441 Huntington Dr., POB 1700, South Pasadena, CA 91030, (800) 525-5959, www.enameling.com

Overglazes
Standard Ceramic Supply, PO Box 4435, Pittsburgh, PA 15205, (412) 923-1655
Thompson Enamel Inc., PO Box 310, Newport, KY 41072

China Paints
Maryland China Company Inc., 54 Main St., Reisterstown, MD 21136-0307, (800) 638-3880
Rynne China Company, 222 W. 8 Mile Rd., Hazel Park, MI 48030, (800) 468-1987

Torches
Wale Apparatus Company Inc., 400 Front St., PO Box D, Hellertown, PA 18055, (800) 334-9253

Safety Glasses
Auralens, (800) 281-2872, www.auralens.com

PMC
PMC Guild, 417 West Mountain Ave., Fort Collins, CO 80521, (970) 419-5503
Rio Grande, 7500 Bluewater Road NW, Albuquerque, NM 87121, (800) 545-6566
PMC Connection, 3718 Cavalier, Garland, TX 75042, (866) 762-2529

Art Clay
Art Clay USA, Inc., 2377 Cranshaw Blvd., Ste. 130, Torrance, CA 90501, (866) 381-0100

Kilns
Paragon Industries, Inc., 2011 South Town East Blvd., Mesquite, TX 75149-1122, (800) 876-4328

Kiln Wires & Repairs
Steve Votta, Rhode Island, (401) 785-8334, Fax (401) 785-8336

Risso Screen & Supplies
Welsh Products, Inc., 932 Grant Ave., Benicia, CA 94510, (800) 745-3255
Dick Blick, Art Materials, PO Box 1267, Galesburg, IL 61402, (800) 933-2542

REFERENCES

The Enamelist Society. *Glass on Metal*, PO Box 631704, Cleveland, Ohio 45263-1704

Thompson Enamel Workbook. Thompson Enamel Inc., PO Box 310, Newport, KY 41072

Untracht, Oppi. *Metal Techniques for Craftsmen*. New York: Doubleday & Company, Inc., 1968

INDEX

A

Acanthus leaves 160
ACC Northeast Craft Fairs 89
acetate 85
acid pickle bath 28, 66, 76, 183
acid, add to water 35, 75, 137
agar 43
Aida Chemical Corp. 179
airbrush 46, 132-133, 153, 167
alkali bath 30
alloy, glass/metal 182
alloys, karat gold 27-31
  melting points of 24
  choosing 29
  problems enameling 30
alloys, nickel 27
alumina hydrate 182
Alundum stones 72, 124, 139, 142
Amacote 69, 70
American Copper & Brass 171
American Craft 103, 104
American Craft Council 106
American Craft Council Northeast Fair 59
American Watercolor Society 100
ammonia 70, 73, 137, 138, 139
annealing 19, 34, 141
appliqués 122
Arizona State University 103
Art Clay 179, 180, 181
Auralens 145

B

Babson Institute 96
Bachrach Art Enamels 89
Bachrach, Lilyan 59-64, 89, 116, 117, 118, 119, 120
baking soda 66, 76, 152
Ball, Fred 108
base coat 19, 21, 25, 33, 41, 45, 54, 59-61, 83, 86, 121-123, 128, 132, 138, 153, 155-156, 164, 167, 172, 181, 183
  firing 48
base metal 147
bàsse-taille 79-83, 159, 183-184

Bates, Kenneth 21, 44, 99, 161
belt sanders 25
bird's nest 66
binders 43 *See also* gum
bisquing 167
bite 138, 184
blistering 160
Blythe C-10 168
Blythe flux 169
Boise State University 100
Bonny Doon Hydraulic Press 155
borax 66
borax-flux 76
boric acid 66, 80
Bradshaw, Sandra E. 65-68, 90
Brannon, Becky 102
bubbling through 52
buffing 34, 73, 77, 135
burnishing 73, 157
butt seam 149

C

cadmium 27, 29, 62
California Institute of Jewelry Training 91
carbo-metho-cellulose 43
Carborundum 77
Carborundum stone 57, 86, 139, 172, 188
Carefree Luster 86, 87
Carnegie-Mellon 99
Carpenter, Woodrow 39-40
cells, enamel 65, 67-68, 72, 75, 79-80
Ceramic Firing Cones 189
ceramic overglazes 59
ceramic pencils 123-125
ceramic pigments 142, 171, 172
cerium oxide 84
chamber, definition of 19
champlevé 33, 40, 75, 79-80, 135, 147
  with Ferric Chloride 101, 135-140
china paints 59, 60, 62
Chinese painting method 62
chlorine gas 137
clarity 39

Cleveland Art Institute 96, 99
cloisonné 25, 37, 51, 57, 59, 65, 75, 83, 147, 152,
    155, 163, 187
    beads 69
    of fine silver 69-73, 91
    jewelry 22, 105, 155
    on copper 107, 163-165, 177
    on fine silver 155-158
    on steel 111, 177-178
Cloisonné Opaque Enamel Jewelry 114, 187-188
cloisonné pendant 55-57
    materials for 56
    procedure for making 56-57
    tools for 56
Cloisonné Wall Pieces on Copper 163-165
cloisons 71, 155
CMC 43, 70, 71
    See also sodium carboxymethylcellulose
coat, definition of 19
collage 85
Color on Metal 103
color palette 62
color sample board 42-43
color samples 182, 187
colored pencils 75
contact firing 121
cooling 81
copper 21, 27, 33, 41, 52, 64, 75, 80, 86-87, 127,
    135, 138-139, 141-142, 147, 151-152, 159,
    163-164, 167-168, 171-172, 175-179, 181,
    183-184, 187
    cleaner 135
    cleaning by buffing wheel 34-35
    cleaning by hand 36-37
    cleaning in acid bath 35-36
    enamel on 121
    forms 60
copper oxide 28
copper sulfate 160
Copper-Glo 135
counter enamel 46, 49, 54, 60-61, 83, 121, 128,
    141, 155, 172, 185
crackle 25, 37, 42, 43, 45, 49, 60, 61, 183
    applying 45-47 *See also* liquid form enamel
Cranbrook Academy of Art 100
Crawford Designs 69
Crawford, Linda 69-73, 91
craze 86

D

Danner, Judy 102
dapping block 70
decals 98, 123-125
Decorative Art Museum 110
Demski, Susan 83, 94
denatured alcohol 187
Denver Art Museum 100
depletion gilded 28
depletion gilding 29-30, 78, 80
design, planning 51
designing, for torch firing 147
direct painting technique 59
dop stick 72
dry sifting 86
dry stencil,
    combined with bubble through 52-53

E

El Camino College 99
electroforming 159
electrolytic stripping 30
electroplating 159
enamel, definition of 19
enamel adhesion, poor 30
enamel adhesive 147
enamel crayons 100, 131-133
enamel discoloration 30
Enamel Guild South 101
enamel piece, definition of 19
enamel watercolor 143
enamel watercolors 133
enameling, definition of 19
enameling copper, problem with 128
enameling oil 121
Enameling on Electroformed Vessels 106, 159-161
Enameling on Sterling Silver 75-78, 92
Enameling Procedure 21
Enameling on Fine Silver Metal Clay 112, 179-182
Enameling: Principles & Practice 21
Enameling Workshop 21
enamels 25
    150 mesh 128
    200 mesh 122, 153
    80 mesh 41, 45, 53, 60, 64, 67, 76, 80, 83, 86,
        121, 123, 128, 138, 141, 147, 152, 153, 160,
        171, 174, 181, 184

enamels *(continued)*
   80 mesh, sifting 48
   applying 43
   composition of 39
   dry 85
   forms of 41
   hard 148
   leaded 39, 67, 80, 128, 147, 152, 160, 164, 171, 180
   manufacture of 39-40
   opalescent 121, 167
   opaque 29, 46, 67, 79, 80, 83, 87, 138, 167, 176
   porcelain 132
   storing 42
   transparent 29, 34, 39, 52, 53, 76, 78, 79, 80, 83, 86, 87, 121, 124, 159, 167, 172, 180, 183, 185
   unleaded 39, 55, 67, 76, 147, 180
   vitreous 187
   washing 42
   wet 175
Enamelwork Supply Co. 171
engraving 79, 183
equipment, enameling 21
   firing 24
   polishing 25
etch 184
etching 135-137, 159, 163, 183
etching bath solution 184
etching ground 138
eutectic 163, 164
eyewear, for safety 145

F

Fashion Institute of Technology 107
Fels Naptha 180
Ferric Chloride 136, 137
Fiberfax 177
filigree 65
filling 68
fines 19, 21
   removing 41
fingerprints 128
finish
   burnished 180
   glossy 135
   high gloss 72, 139
   matte 77, 124, 139, 180
   satin 169, 180, 182
   semi-gloss 139
fire gilding 28
fire, optimum 40
fired, definition of 19
firescale 19, 33, 35, 51-52, 76, 86, 123, 135, 139, 168, 171, 172, 185
firescale inhibitor 69, 70, 123, 138
firing 21, 29, 34, 41, 52, 59, 61, 67, 68, 72, 80, 81, 83, 87, 125, 128, 133, 135, 138, 143, 147, 151, 153, 156, 158, 160, 164, 167
firing fork 23
firing process 48-49
firing rack 19 *See also* planche
firing range 39
firing setup 61, 69
firing station 146
firing temperature 39
firing times 145
firing, healthy 19
firings 53, 85
fixative, inorganic 123
flash firing 19, 84
flowing 53
flux 19, 34, 40, 41, 43, 48, 49, 52, 54, 59-61, 66, 70, 77, 83, 122, 124, 128, 139, 142, 149, 152, 155, 156, 159, 168, 171, 172, 176, 178, 183
foils 34, 121-122, 138, 157, 169, 171-172
   copper 159
   gold 86, 121-122, 139
   silver 121-122
Foils: Fine Silver and 24k Gold 97, 121-122
Foley, Alexa P. 75-78, 92
fork 19
Friedman, Edward J. 21, 79-82, 93
frit 39
fumes 136
   toxic 152
Fusager, Falcher 83-84, 94
fusing 41, 77, 86-87, 122, 128
   process 152
   time 124
fusion 124

G

gas porosity 31
gauge 33

gesso 167
glass-etch 169
glazes 123
gloss 39
gold 27-31, 41, 69, 79, 83, 155, 157-158, 171, 179, 180, 182, 184, 187-188
Gold Alloy Enameling 93
Gold Alloys 27-31, 79-82
Gold Cloisonné Wire On Fine Silver 83-84, 94
gold, melting points 27
Gore, Jenny 85-87, 95
graphite 174
grinding 25, 63, 156, 157
Grice, Stuart 27-31
Grisaille 109, 122, 171-172
ground coat 131, 132
grout 129
grout sealer 129
gum, enameling 19, 34, 37, 43, 48, 52, 54, 86, 128

H

Hall, Doris 45, 51, 54, 61, 89, 96
hammock 19, 183
Handy Flux 152
Harper, William 115
heat treat 29
heating 148
Hercules Powder Co. 128
Hiroshima City 110
Hoover & Strong Inc. 27, 29, 93
Hunter, Marianne 97, 121-122

I

Indian Jewelry Supply 152
Indian Sand Painting 19, 45, 53
indium 27
ink 63
iron 131
iron, enameling 131, 132
IT solder 76, 152

J

Japanese flux 169
Japanese leaded enamels 152, 158
Japanese lotus root powder 153

Japanese opalescents 168
Jasen, June E. 98, 123-125
Jeffrey, Charles 22
Jenkins, Jean Foster 34, 42, 43, 99, 127-129
jewelry 33, 36, 59, 75, 83, 121-122, 135-136, 146, 155, 171-172, 187
jewels 79
jump ring 55, 78, 79, 135

K

Killmaster, John 100, 131-133
kiln 19, 21, 23, 163
   electric 69, 77
   Firemaster 155
   home-made 132
   Norman 20, 60, 177
   Trinket 21, 121
   Vcella 168
kiln dimensions 22
kiln furniture 61
kiln temperature 48, 189
kiln wash 22
Klyr-Fyre 43, 46, 47, 48, 67, 77, 83, 86, 123, 138, 139, 142, 143, 153, 155, 156, 160, 164, 168, 169, 172, 177
Klyr-Koat 183
Komrad, Audrey 101, 135-140
Kubinyi, Kalman 43, 54, 96
Kulicke, Bob 114
Kuller, Ora K. 102, 141-144
Kunstgewerbe Museum 106

L

La Rocco, Anthony 120
Lang, Marian 115
lap seam 149
lapidary equipment 156
Large Mosaic Enamels 99, 127-129
Laskin, Rebecca 102
lavender oil, imitation 172
layering 52, 84
Layering Over Sgraffitoed Liquid Enamel Base Coat 108, 167-169
Lea Compound C 34-36, 60, 135
Limoges 40, 109, 171
Limoges Museum of Enamels 110

liquation, partial 31
liquid enamel 132
Liquid Flux 183, 184
Liquid Flux as Etching Resist for Bàsse-Taille 113, 183-185
liquid flux, unfired 183
liquid form enamel 25, 54 *See also* crackle
    applying 45
Lozier, Deborah 21, 103, 145-150
lump 39
lumps 54
luster 82
luster effect 160
lusters 125

M

Magick/Fusager-Demski Design 83-84, 94
marks 27
marquette 127
masking 142
matte-salts 124-125
maturity 19, 61, 71, 77, 81, 121, 132, 139, 153, 185
melt point 31
Mendocino Jewelry Gallery 91
mesh, definition of 19
metal clay 179-182
Metal Gauges and Weights 189
Metal Melting Point 189
Metal Techniques for Craftsmen 159
Metalsmith 103, 104
Metropolitan Museum of Art 106
mezuzahs 59
Micro-Mark 163
mineral spirits 136
Miniature Paintings 171-172
Mitsubishi Materials Corp. 179
modeling 122
Mosaic Enamels 127-129
mosaic, indoor 129
Mosan 40
muffle, definition of 19

N

New York University 101
Newark Art Museum 107
nibbler 163
nickel 27

Ninomiya N1 Flux 71, 181
nitric acid 30, 35, 75-76, 137, 184
nitric acid bath 80

O

Oakland Museum 103
opacity 39
opaque 178
opaques 42, 85, 145, 149, 161, 185
    lead-bearing 40
    lead-free 168
orange peel stage 19, 121, 138, 168
organic oxides 123
Origami 179
ornament 103-104
OSHA 40
overglaze color 64
Overglaze Direct Painting 59-64, 89
Overglaze Painting Color 142
overglazes 25, 59, 60
    painting with 41
    transparent 63
oxidation 27
oxide scale 82
oxides 30, 148

P

packing 84
painting 62, 142
painting enamels 87
Painting Flux 142
paisley design 54-55, 96
    procedure 54-55
palladium 27
pantograph 127
patterns 163
pendants 79, 138, 171, 179, 187
Penny-Brite® copper cleaner 25, 36, 60, 141
Perkins, Sarah 43, 104, 151-153
petri dish 25, 60, 62
Philadelphia College of Art 111
photo silk-screen 173
photocopies 141
pickle 27-28, 35, 75-76, 80-81, 123, 128, 152
pickling 30
pickling acid 30

picklings 27
pigments, ceramic 39
planche 19, 22, 24, 172
plaques 135
plating, gold 140
platinum 79
plique-à-jour 65-68, 75, 78, 90, 147
PMC 179-182 *See also* Precious Metal Clay
polishing 68, 72, 140
porcelain slip 45
Portrait With Enamel Watercolors 102, 141-44
portraits 141
potassium nitrate 39
Precious Metal Clay 179-182 *See also* PMC
Precious Metal Clay-Silver Enameling 112
pulling through 53
pumice 187
pyrometer 19, 22, 40, 60, 69, 83, 128, 132, 155, 163, 177
   digital 67

Q

quenching 28, 80

R

Rae, Merry-Lee 105, 155-158
raku 160
refilling 81
Renwick Gallery 106
repoussé 33, 131
resist 136-138, 183
rheostat 48, 83, 128
rims, attached 152
rings 79, 171
Risso Screen 110, 173-176
roll quenched 39
Russian soldering method 65-68, 90
   See also plique-à-jour
rust 131
Ryan, John 90

S

San Diego Enamel Guild 113
San Diego State University 94, 104, 173
San Diego University 110
Scalex 43, 123, 138, 139, 142

Schwarcz, June 106, 159-161
Schwarcz, Leroy 159
screening, dry 175
sgraffito 25, 42, 47, 51-52, 57, 61, 86-87, 133, 136, 142, 167-168, 176, 183
Shears 25, 83, 171, 177
Sheffield College of Arts and Crafts 111
sifters, making 43-44
sifting 19, 21, 25, 44, 61, 85, 121, 128, 141, 171
   methods of 44, 48-49
silk-screen 123, 133, 173
silver 21, 28, 33, 41, 55, 69, 78, 135-136, 141, 151, 157, 163, 177-182, 187-188
   solder 76
   cleaning 37
   enamel on 121
sintering 179-181
Slepian, Marian 107, 163-165
Smithsonian 100
smoothness 39
Sobo white glue 65
soda ash 39
sodium bicarbonate 30
sodium carboxymethylcellulose 70 *See also* CMC
solder 31, 66, 79, 145, 149-151
soldering 29, 66, 79-80
soldering flux 70, 75
Southern Illinois University 104
Southwest Missouri State University 104
Sparex 2 35, 36, 66, 70, 75, 76, 80, 81, 128, 131, 135, 138, 139, 159, 160, 168
speed screen 173
spray gun 132
spraying 19, 21
stains 123
Standard Ceramic Supply Co. 59
steamer 81
steel 33, 41, 131
   plaques 177
   plate 65
stencils 85-87
Stencils and Watercolors 85-87, 95
stencils, wet 53
sterling silver 72, 75
sterling silver oxide 76
stilt 19, 61
   Atlas ceramic 24
   bed-of-nails 128

Stone, Joanna 92
Stone, Judy 52, 108, 167-169
stoning 77, 81, 139
stresses 67
sulfuric acid 27, 30, 159
sulfuric acid bath 160
supplies, enameling 21
sweat solder 75
Swiss method 57
switch covers 167
switch plates 59
Szabados, Alex 109, 171, 172
Szabados, Mona 109, 171-172

T

T.B. Hagstoz and Sons, Inc. 66
tack welding 150
Tanzer, JoAnn 110, 173-176
The Buehn Company 93
The Enamelist Society 101, 104
The Revere Academy of Jewelry Arts 93
thermal expansion 39
thermal screen 173
Thermofax 175
Thompson Enamel Company 59, 66, 131, 141
Thompson Enamel Workbook 33
Thompson's catalog 41
Timofeev, Valeri 90
tin 27
tongs 36
    rule for using 36
torch 69, 81
    set-up 146
    jeweler's 65
    Meco Midget 70
torch firing 103, 145-150
    designing for 147
    tools for 145
torching 80
tragacanth 43
transferring 123
transparents 42, 121, 138, 145, 147, 149, 151, 152, 161, 164, 168, 171, 176, 185
Trippetti, Joseph 56, 89, 107, 111, 116, 177-178
trivet 19, 23, 83, 121, 135, 171, 183
tubing 72
typing paper 25

U

UCLA 99
ultrasonic bath 30
underbite 136, 137
undercoat 33
Untracht, Oppi 159

V

Vessel Forms 104, 151-153
Vistafax 173
vocabulary, enamelist's 19
Vormelker, Jean 112, 179-182

W

Wale Apparatus Company 146
Wallen, Phyllis 113, 183-185
watercolor 125, 133
    technique 87
watercolors 62, 87, 131-133, 141-143
wax 72, 136, 138, 159
Weber's Liquid Etching Ground 136
wet inlay 86
wet pack 62, 64, 77, 152-153, 157, 187
wet packing 19, 21, 25, 44, 51, 128, 164, 172, 180
    tools for 44
wet stencils 53
wet-inlay 160
wet-lay 80
Whitney, Ginny 114, 187-188
Who's Who in American Art 100
Who's Who in the West 100
wire
    cloisonné 34, 55, 69, 71, 75, 77, 83-84, 138-139, 152-153, 155-158, 163-164, 177-178, 187
    gold 77
    kiln 22-24
    silver 65
Worcester Art Museum School 89
Worcester Center for Crafts 89
workshop, enameling 21-25

Z

zinc 27, 28, 29, 79
zinc oxide 28

Enameling with Professionals was printed in a limited edition of 1,000. The text was set by Julie Murkette, Hardwick, Massachusetts in Galliard and Eras typefaces. The book was printed by Mercantile/Image Press, Inc., West Boylston, Massachusetts on Scheufelen Phoeno Star dull coated paper, and bound by Acme Bookbinding, Charlestown, Massachusetts.